W9-CAR-671

MODERN WORLD LEADERS

Pope John Paul II

MODERN WORLD LEADERS

Tony Blair
George W. Bush
Hugo Chávez
Pope Benedict XVI
Pope John Paul II
The Saudi Royal Family
Vladimir Putin

MODERN WORLD LEADERS

Pope John Paul II

Edward J. Renehan, Jr.

CHELSEA HOUSE
PUBLISHERS
An imprint of Infobase Publishing

Pope John Paul II

Copyright © 2007 by Infobase Publishing

All rights reserved. No part of this book may be reproduced or utilized in any form or by any means, electronic or mechanical, including photocopying, recording, or by any information storage or retrieval systems, without permission in writing from the publisher. For information, contact:

Chelsea House
An imprint of Infobase Publishing
132 West 31st Street
New York, NY 10001

Library of Congress Cataloging-in-Publication Data

Renehan, Edward, 1956–
  Pope John Paul II / Edward J. Renehan, Jr.
    p. cm. — (Modern world leaders)
  Includes bibliographical references and index.
  ISBN 0-7910-9227-5 (hardcover)
  1. John Paul II, Pope, 1920–2005—Juvenile literature. 2. Popes—Biography—Juvenile literature. I. Title. II. Series.
  BX1378.5.R46 2006
  282.092—dc22   2006010612

Chelsea House books are available at special discounts when purchased in bulk quantities for businesses, associations, institutions, or sales promotions. Please call our Special Sales Department in New York at (212) 967-8800 or (800) 322-8755.

You can find Chelsea House on the World Wide Web at http://www.chelseahouse.com

Text design by Erik Lindstrom
Cover design by Takeshi Takahashi

Printed in the United States of America

Bang FOF 10 9 8 7 6 5 4 3 2 1

This book is printed on acid-free paper.

All links and Web addresses were checked and verified to be correct at the time of publication. Because of the dynamic nature of the Web, some addresses and links may have changed since publication and may no longer be valid.

TABLE OF CONTENTS

ARTHUR M. SCHLESINGER, JR.

On Leadership

Leadership, it may be said, is really what makes the world go round. Love no doubt smoothes the passage; but love is a private transaction between consenting adults. Leadership is a public transaction with history. The idea of leadership affirms the capacity of individuals to move, inspire, and mobilize masses of people so that they act together in pursuit of an end. Sometimes leadership serves good purposes, sometimes bad; but whether the end is benign or evil, great leaders are those men and women who leave their personal stamp on history.

Now, the very concept of leadership implies the proposition that individuals can make a difference. This proposition has never been universally accepted. From classical times to the present day, eminent thinkers have regarded individuals as no more than the agents and pawns of larger forces, whether the gods and goddesses of the ancient world or, in the modern era, race, class, nation, the dialectic, the will of the people, the spirit of the times, history itself. Against such forces, the individual dwindles into insignificance.

So contends the thesis of historical determinism. Tolstoy's great novel *War and Peace* offers a famous statement of the case. Why, Tolstoy asked, did millions of men in the Napoleonic Wars, denying their human feelings and their common sense, move back and forth across Europe slaughtering their fellows? "The war," Tolstoy answered, "was bound to happen simply because it was bound to happen." All prior history determined it. As for leaders, they, Tolstoy said, "are but the labels that serve to give a name to an end and, like labels, they have the least possible connection with the event." The greater the leader, "the more conspicuous the inevitability and the predestination of every act he commits." The leader, said Tolstoy, is "the slave of history."

Determinism takes many forms. Marxism is the determinism of class. Nazism the determinism of race. But the idea of men and women as the slaves of history runs athwart the deepest human instincts. Rigid determinism abolishes the idea of human freedom—the assumption of free choice that underlies every move we make, every word we speak, every thought we think. It abolishes the idea of human responsibility, since it is manifestly unfair to reward or punish people for actions that are by definition beyond their control. No one can live consistently by any deterministic creed. The Marxist states prove this themselves by their extreme susceptibility to the cult of leadership.

More than that, history refutes the idea that individuals make no difference. In December 1931, a British politician crossing Fifth Avenue in New York City between 76th and 77th streets around 10:30 P.M. looked in the wrong direction and was knocked down by an automobile—a moment, he later recalled, of a man aghast, a world aglare: "I do not understand why I was not broken like an eggshell or squashed like a gooseberry." Fourteen months later an American politician, sitting in an open car in Miami, Florida, was fired on by an assassin; the man beside him was hit. Those who believe that individuals make no difference to history might well ponder whether the next two decades would have been the same had Mario Constasino's car killed Winston Churchill in 1931 and Giuseppe Zangara's bullet killed Franklin Roosevelt in 1933. Suppose, in addition, that Lenin had died of typhus in Siberia in 1895 and that Hitler had been killed on the western front in 1916. What would the twentieth century have looked like now?

For better or for worse, individuals do make a difference. "The notion that a people can run itself and its affairs anonymously," wrote the philosopher William James, "is now well known to be the silliest of absurdities. Mankind does nothing save through initiatives on the part of inventors, great or small, and imitation by the rest of us—these are the sole factors in human progress. Individuals of genius show the way, and set the patterns, which common people then adopt and follow."

Leadership, James suggests, means leadership in thought as well as in action. In the long run, leaders in thought may well make the greater difference to the world. "The ideas of economists and political philosophers, both when they are right and when they are wrong," wrote John Maynard Keynes, "are more powerful than is commonly understood. Indeed the world is ruled by little else. Practical men, who believe themselves to be quite exempt from any intellectual influences, are usually the slaves of some defunct economist. . . . The power of vested interests is vastly exaggerated compared with the gradual encroachment of ideas."

But, as Woodrow Wilson once said, "Those only are leaders of men, in the general eye, who lead in action. . . . It is at their hands that new thought gets its translation into the crude language of deeds." Leaders in thought often invent in solitude and obscurity, leaving to later generations the tasks of imitation. Leaders in action—the leaders portrayed in this series—have to be effective in their own time.

And they cannot be effective by themselves. They must act in response to the rhythms of their age. Their genius must be adapted, in a phrase from William James, "to the receptivities of the moment." Leaders are useless without followers. "There goes the mob," said the French politician, hearing a clamor in the streets. "I am their leader. I must follow them." Great leaders turn the inchoate emotions of the mob to purposes of their own. They seize on the opportunities of their time, the hopes, fears, frustrations, crises, potentialities. They succeed when events have prepared the way for them, when the community is awaiting to be aroused, when they can provide the clarifying and organizing ideas. Leadership completes the circuit between the individual and the mass and thereby alters history.

It may alter history for better or for worse. Leaders have been responsible for the most extravagant follies and most monstrous crimes that have beset suffering humanity. They have also been vital in such gains as humanity has made in individual freedom, religious and racial tolerance, social justice, and respect for human rights.

There is no sure way to tell in advance who is going to lead for good and who for evil. But a glance at the gallery of men and women in MODERN WORLD LEADERS suggests some useful tests.

One test is this: Do leaders lead by force or by persuasion? By command or by consent? Through most of history leadership was exercised by the divine right of authority. The duty of followers was to defer and to obey. "Theirs not to reason why/Theirs but to do and die." On occasion, as with the so-called enlightened despots of the eighteenth century in Europe, absolutist leadership was animated by humane purposes. More often, absolutism nourished the passion for domination, land, gold, and conquest and resulted in tyranny.

The great revolution of modern times has been the revolution of equality. "Perhaps no form of government," wrote the British historian James Bryce in his study of the United States, *The American Commonwealth*, "needs great leaders so much as democracy." The idea that all people should be equal in their legal condition has undermined the old structure of authority, hierarchy, and deference. The revolution of equality has had two contrary effects on the nature of leadership. For equality, as Alexis de Tocqueville pointed out in his great study *Democracy in America*, might mean equality in servitude as well as equality in freedom.

"I know of only two methods of establishing equality in the political world," Tocqueville wrote. "Rights must be given to every citizen, or none at all to anyone . . . save one, who is the master of all." There was no middle ground "between the sovereignty of all and the absolute power of one man." In his astonishing prediction of twentieth-century totalitarian dictatorship, Tocqueville explained how the revolution of equality could lead to the *Führerprinzip* and more terrible absolutism than the world had ever known.

But when rights are given to every citizen and the sovereignty of all is established, the problem of leadership takes a new form, becomes more exacting than ever before. It is easy to issue commands and enforce them by the rope and the stake, the concentration camp and the *gulag*. It is much harder to use argument and achievement to overcome opposition and win consent. The Founding Fathers of the United States understood the difficulty. They believed that history had given them the opportunity to decide, as Alexander Hamilton wrote in the first Federalist Paper, whether men are indeed capable of basing government on "reflection and choice, or whether they are forever destined to depend . . . on accident and force."

Government by reflection and choice called for a new style of leadership and a new quality of followership. It required leaders to be responsive to popular concerns, and it required followers to be active and informed participants in the process. Democracy does not eliminate emotion from politics; sometimes it fosters demagoguery; but it is confident that, as the greatest of democratic leaders put it, you cannot fool all of the people all of the time. It measures leadership by results and retires those who overreach or falter or fail.

It is true that in the long run despots are measured by results too. But they can postpone the day of judgment, sometimes indefinitely, and in the meantime they can do infinite harm. It is also true that democracy is no guarantee of virtue and intelligence in government, for the voice of the people is not necessarily the voice of God. But democracy, by assuring the right of opposition, offers built-in resistance to the evils inherent in absolutism. As the theologian Reinhold Niebuhr summed it up, "Man's capacity for justice makes democracy possible, but man's inclination to justice makes democracy necessary."

A second test for leadership is the end for which power is sought. When leaders have as their goal the supremacy of a master race or the promotion of totalitarian revolution or the acquisition and exploitation of colonies or the protection of greed and privilege or the preservation of personal power, it is likely that their leadership will do little to advance the cause of humanity. When their goal is the abolition of slavery, the liberation of women, the enlargement of opportunity for the poor and powerless, the extension of equal rights to racial minorities, the defense of the freedoms of expression and opposition, it is likely that their leadership will increase the sum of human liberty and welfare.

Leaders have done great harm to the world. They have also conferred great benefits. You will find both sorts in this series. Even "good" leaders must be regarded with a certain wariness. Leaders are not demigods; they put on their trousers one leg after another just like ordinary mortals. No leader is infallible, and every leader needs to be reminded of this at regular intervals. Irreverence irritates leaders but is their salvation. Unquestioning submission corrupts leaders and demeans followers. Making a cult of a leader is always a mistake. Fortunately hero worship generates its own antidote. "Every hero," said Emerson, "becomes a bore at last."

The single benefit the great leaders confer is to embolden the rest of us to live according to our own best selves, to be active, insistent, and resolute in affirming our own sense of things. For great leaders attest to the reality of human freedom against the supposed inevitabilities of history. And they attest to the wisdom and power that may lie within the most unlikely of us, which is why Abraham Lincoln remains the supreme example of great leadership. A great leader, said Emerson, exhibits new possibilities to all humanity. "We feed on genius. . . . Great men exist that there may be greater men."

Great leaders, in short, justify themselves by emancipating and empowering their followers. So humanity struggles to master its destiny, remembering with Alexis de Tocqueville: "It is true that around every man a fatal circle is traced beyond which he cannot pass; but within the wide verge of that circle he is powerful and free; as it is with man, so with communities." ●

1

The Death of a Pope

THROUGH THE DAY ON APRIL 2, 2005, POPE JOHN PAUL II—THE 264TH MAN in history to serve as bishop of Rome and therefore leader to the world's more than one billion Catholics—lay dying in the Apostolic Palace at the heart of the Vatican. The 84-year-old pontiff—current holder of the throne of St. Peter, Christ's favorite apostle and the first bishop of Rome—lay still under white sheets. John Paul's head tilted slightly to one side of his pillow. His eyes looked out half-knowingly from the tight slits of nearly closed lids. And his lungs worked slowly, unevenly, struggling to keep up the rhythm they'd maintained so effortlessly in the past, even after John Paul was felled by shots from a would-be assassin in St. Peter's Square (a man whom he subsequently met with and forgave) in 1981.

As the pope labored toward his final moments, commentators and pundits worldwide began to take stock of John Paul's life and papacy, and his impact on both his church and his world.

Editorial writers recalled the boy from the poor Polish town: the onetime poet and playwright who loved the woodlands more than he loved nearly anything else, but who nevertheless found himself elevated to head the Roman Catholic Church in October 1978. The Right Reverend Billy Graham—high-profile leader of American Protestants—described the dying man as "unquestionably the most influential voice for morality and peace in the world during the last 100 years." Bono, lead singer for the Irish rock band U2, spoke of John Paul reverentially, without a hint of sarcasm, as "the best frontman the Catholic Church ever had." (In a way, it was appropriate that the likes of Bono should comment, for John Paul—the first pope of the modern information age—had been as much a celebrity as he'd been a religious leader.) Holocaust survivor and Nobel Peace Prize winner Elie Wiesel told reporters that John Paul "will have a very important place in Jewish history" as the first pope to visit a synagogue. "Never have the relations between Jews and Catholics been as good," Wiesel added. And the pope's onetime nemesis, former Soviet leader Mikhail Gorbachev, praised him as well, remembering how John Paul once told him the Soviet bloc must be freed so that Europe could "breathe with both its lungs." At the same time, human-rights advocates remembered how this pope had made numerous trips to the third world, agitated loudly against the death penalty, and vainly did his best to warn the "first world" against the dangers of materialism, consumerism, and nihilism.

But not all was praise. Some writers and broadcasters voiced criticism tempered with respect. Experts on American television noted John Paul's seeming hesitancy to respond to the priest pedophilia scandals. Activists and reformers within the church complained about John Paul's strict conservatism on matters of faith, particularly his unwillingness to evolve and modernize on key issues like birth control, abortion, divorce, homosexuality, marriage for priests, and the notion of women in the priesthood. It was as a result of John Paul's dogmatism on these topics, they argued, that the European church seemed stagnant. (For example, the number of priests ordained in Dublin, Ireland, during all of 2004 came to a grand total of just *one*.) Fans of the pope countered, however, that the church had expanded greatly worldwide during John Paul's tenure, especially in Latin America, Africa, and throughout the rest of the developing world. "The center of the Catholic Church has moved beyond Western Europe," noted John Haldane, an expert on Catholicism and a professor at Scotland's University of St. Andrews. "[John Paul II] was really a Pope for the world, not just for the Church."

Partisan bickering ended once the pope breathed his last breath. Cardinal Achille Silvestrini, 81, a former Vatican diplomat and good friend to the pope, held John Paul's hand as the pontiff calmly reached his end that evening of Saturday, April 2. Silvestrini told reporters later that, just a moment before the pope's death, he and the pontiff had been listening to a Mass down in St. Peter's Square broadcast via a public address system. At 9:37 P.M. exactly, following the end of a prayer recited by a priest down in the square, the pope muttered, "Amen," and then took his last breath. With that he passed into history and—some argued—sainthood.

John Paul's personal physician, Dr. Renato Buzzonetti, used an EKG machine to produce a flat-line electrocardiogram, thus confirming the death. (In previous centuries, death was traditionally confirmed by tapping the papal brow three times with a silver hammer, but for the twenty-first century, a more modern method was adopted.) After the EKG formality, a light linen cloth was placed over the pontiff's face. Then, in a centuries-old tradition, the Spanish cardinal Eduardo Martinez Somalo, Vatican chamberlain, repeatedly called the pope's given name, Karol, as the pope's signet "fisherman's ring," which each pope uses to seal correspondence, was removed and taken away to be ceremonially crushed. Once these steps were accomplished, at 10 P.M. exactly, Archbishop Leonardo Sandri—the man who most

Cardinals bow in tribute to Pope John Paul II at his funeral on April 8, 2005, in Vatican City. Karol Wojtyla became the 264th leader of the Catholic Church and held the papacy from 1978 to 2005.

often filled in for the pope in his later years, as John Paul's strength slowly failed him—announced the news to the thousands gathered at St. Peter's Square. "The Pope has returned to the house of our Father." As Sandri spoke, fellow cardinals symbolically sealed the doors to John Paul's quarters using ribbons and red wax of the type generally used to seal Vatican correspondence.

In the days that followed, a strict formula of tribute and funereal protocol was to be applied. Tradition dictated six days of mourning, including four days of public viewing beneath the dome of St. Peter's, followed by a funeral Mass lasting several hours, held outdoors in St. Peter's Square. After all that, John Paul would be interred in the ancient vaulted crypt below the sanctuary, there to join 147 of his predecessors. (Specifically, Vatican insiders confided to the press, John Paul would be placed in the marble tomb previously occupied by Pope John XXIII, whose remains were moved after he was beatified by John Paul in 2000.) The pope's body, unembalmed, was to be placed in three nesting caskets made of cypress, lead, and elm, these symbolizing John Paul's humanity, his death, and his dignity. With the body would go the remains of John Paul's signet ring, a death certificate, and Vatican coins minted during his papacy.

The pope died on a Saturday. The following Monday, his body was carried from the Apostolic Palace, through St. Peter's Square, to the basilica. A group of priests headed the procession. They cast their eyes down to the ground and solemnly chanted the *Litany of Saints*. The hushed throng listened in silence to the somber intonations. Some of those present wept; others smiled with joy at the thought of their pontiff achieving his reward with Christ in Heaven. Most of the College of Cardinals of the Roman Catholic Church followed the priest in the procession. Behind the cardinals, in slow lockstep, walked the so-called "Papal Gentlemen" in their gray tailcoats and white gloves. The gentlemen carried a scarlet platform atop their shoulders. On that platform rested the robed and serene body of John Paul. Within the basilica, the Papal gentlemen laid down the body for viewing.

The doors opened shortly before 8 P.M. that Monday, more than an hour before the Vatican had said they would

IN THE END, 4 KINGS, 5 QUEENS,
AT LEAST 70 PRESIDENTS AND PRIME
MINISTERS, AND MORE THAN
14 LEADERS OF OTHER RELIGIONS
GATHERED TO JOIN 300,000
MOURNERS IN ST. PETER'S SQUARE.

open. Thereafter, a steady flow of mourners filed past the body, with some crossing themselves or taking photos as they walked alongside a red, waist-high barrier about ten feet from the body. The basilica closed at 3 A.M., Tuesday, and then reopened about 4:40 A.M., a few minutes ahead of the scheduled time of 5 A.M. From that time on, the basilica remained open 22 hours per day until the pope's Friday funeral.

Throughout that period, long lines wound out of the Vatican and through the streets of Rome, sojourners and faithful from around the world waiting to gaze upon the pope one last time. More than 4 million such visitors were expected throughout the solemn days of mourning. "What broke my heart was knowing with each step I was closer to seeing him no longer alive," remembered Linda Baustamante, 19, of Texas. "But when I saw him so peaceful, my tears dried up." Another woman, Marta Gakh of the Ukraine, carried her 11-month-old son. "He'll never remember this," she told a reporter, referring to her baby, "but I will remind him and he will know that he was able to say goodbye to the Pope that loved children so much." "This is a pilgrimage," said another mourner, 21-year-old Giovanna Ienco, of the throngs who converged on the cobblestones of St. Peter's Square. "He is already a saint."

In the end, 4 kings, 5 queens, at least 70 presidents and prime ministers, and more than 14 leaders of other religions gathered to join 300,000 mourners in St. Peter's Square for the Friday funeral. These included President George W. Bush of the United States, his two predecessors (Bill Clinton and George H.W. Bush), and even the presidents of Iran and Syria, governments on the U.S. State Department's list of terrorism supporters. Britain's Prince Charles postponed his wedding for a day in order to attend, in partnership with British Prime Minister Tony Blair. Never had so many world leaders come together for the funeral of a religious leader. Never had such a funeral drawn the interest of so many. Across Rome, hundreds of thousands of additional mourners gathered in soccer fields and old Roman arenas to watch the proceedings on large television monitors. Around the world, television viewership broke records. The Rev. Michael Driscoll, who teaches liturgy at the University of Notre Dame, said that although the 1978 funerals of Popes Paul VI and John Paul I were televised, "it was nothing like this. This is almost like a made-for-media event. We're glued to the set." Philadelphia cardinal Justin Rigali, who was at St. Peter's for three previous papal funerals, called the outpouring for John Paul II the most dramatic he's ever seen: "This exceeds everything."

At the center of all the pomp and pageantry lay the body of John Paul II dressed in liturgical vestments: a white miter on his head, a set of rosary beads in his folded hands, and a shepherd's stick topped by a crucifix under one arm.

On the day of the funeral in St. Peter's Square, the papal gentlemen slowly carried the body—now encased in the first of the three coffins in which it would be placed—out from the basilica and into the tearful yet jubilant crowd, an assembly that seemed "Catholic" in the broadest sense of the term. Here were Croatian students, Filipina nuns, American teenagers, Chinese refugees. Some held banners that praised John Paul as "Our angel." Church groups waved colorful handkerchiefs; Polish nationals waved their country's flag in honor of their native son.

A cross and the letter M, for Mary, were laminated on the lid of the coffin. As the casket emerged from the basilica, a papal

On the day of Pope John Paul's funeral, St. Peter's Square overflowed with people paying their respects. Whether they were present or watched on television, billions of people viewed the funeral, which was followed by nine days of mourning.

aide placed a volume of the Gospels open on top, allowing the pages to blow symbolically in the wind. Then the gray-clad gentlemen moved toward the spot before the altar where they would place the box, and the Vatican's Sistine Choir chanted in Latin, "Lord, grant him eternal rest." In the midst of the long Mass that followed, Cardinal Joseph Ratzinger—a German, the dean of the College of Cardinals, one of John Paul's closest aides and associates, and a man (as many might have guessed) headed for the papacy himself—delivered a homily in which he eulogized John Paul but also noted the work that lay unfinished. Recalling the highlights of John Paul's life dating from his boyhood, Ratzinger focused on the sacrifices John Paul made for the church. At the same time, Ratzinger summoned his listeners to be equally selfless: to work for the faith on all fronts, not to be lulled into complacency by the easy comforts of Western affluence, to evade the wiles of wealth and selfishness. "[John Paul] realized how true are the Lord's words: Those who try to make their life secure lose it. . . . Today, we bury his remains in the earth as a seed of immortality—our hearts are full of sadness, yet at the same time of joyful hope and profound gratitude."

As Ratzinger spoke, television cameras panned the most illustrious of his listeners. It seemed that even in death, John Paul II had the power to heal wounds and inspire peace, at least momentarily. Kings of Christian countries such as Spain stood side by side with Muslim leaders like President Mohammad Khatami of Iran. Meanwhile, the president of Israel, Moshe Katzav, sat just a few rows in front of Bashar Assad, president of Syria, even though the two countries remained officially at war.

After the conclusion of Ratzinger's remarks and the end of the Mass, the twelve papal gentlemen lifted the cypress coffin and carried it toward the basilica's "Door of the Dead." Then, just short of the door and in a last gesture to the throng, the men slowly turned the coffin so that the good shepherd, the pope, could face his flock one last time, and they him. Instantly came the cries from thousands: *Giovanni Paolo! Santo Subito!* John Paul! Sainthood at once! After this, in a heartbeat, the gray-clad gentlemen moved as one through the large door, removing John Paul from public view forever. But even after his coffin had disappeared, the crowd was unwilling to let go. The people applauded for a full ten minutes as the knell of

Cardinal Joseph Ratzinger, who would succeed John Paul II in the papacy, blesses the body of his good friend and mentor. Ratzinger was elected eleven days after the funeral of John Paul II, taking the name Benedict XVI.

the basilica's ten-ton bell was joined by chimes from steeples throughout Rome, Catholic and Protestant alike.

The ceremonies still had a short way to go, however. Within the ancient silence of St. Peter's, beyond the reach of television cameras and away from the cheers of the square, a long line of scarlet-robed cardinals formed a somber honor guard down both sides of the aisle leading to the crypt. The cardinals doffed their *zucchetti* (skullcaps) in tribute, as the pope's remains passed each man. "It was total silence," recalled Cardinal Roger Mahony of Los Angeles. "After the Holy Father had passed by and everybody left and were out of sight, we turned to go back and take off our vestments, and no one said a word. Not a word."

A handful of the pope's closest colleagues accompanied the coffin into the crypt. Now, deep in the bowels of the basilica, came the two additional coffins. Cardinal Somalo performed yet another brief service, this concluding with the same words that opened the funeral: "Lord, grant him eternal rest, and may perpetual light shine upon him." Then those gathered lowered Pope John Paul II down into his grave, the final earthly stop on a long road that had begun so many years before, in Poland.

CHAPTER

Early Years

THE BOY DESTINED TO BECOME POPE JOHN PAUL II WAS BORN IN 1920, and he first saw the light of this world in a small town called Wadowice, 35 miles southwest of Krakow in Poland. Eight thousand Catholics lived there; so did 2,000 Jews. Karol Wojtyla (pronounced voy-TIH-wah) bore the same name as his father, a retired army officer and tailor. The boy's mother, Emilia Kaczorowska Wojtyla, was a schoolteacher of Lithuanian descent. Karol also had one much older brother, Edmund, a physician and the pride of the family, whom he looked up to, admired, and loved dearly. (An infant sister had died before Karol was born.)

Karol's parents were strict and devout Catholics but notable in that they did not share the anti-Semitic views of many other Polish Catholics. Many of Karol's boyhood friends were Jews. (Years later, in October 1978, the newly named Pope John Paul II would give his very first private Vatican audience not to a fellow Catholic, but to his boyhood pal and lifelong friend Jerzy Kluger, one of the few members of Wadowice's Jewish population to survive the Holocaust. Eleven years later, the pope asked Kluger to represent him at the unveiling of the commemorative plaque on the site of the destroyed Wadowice synagogue.)

Living in the same neighborhood, the two boys played together often as young children. Later they sat side by side in the local elementary school. In an interview given two years before the death of the pope, Kluger related how he and "Lolek"—as Karol was called by his closest friends—had shared a singular curiosity about the police officer charged with patrolling Wadowice. They wanted to know whether the ceremonial sword that the man wore was real or, as they suspected, wooden. One day, the two little boys caught the policeman napping. It was now that they drew the sword partially out of its scabbard to satisfy their curiosity, but a moment later the policeman awoke and caught them in the act. (The sword was real but, fortunately, the good-natured policeman's outrage was not.)

Jerzy's father, an attorney, was the president of Wadowice's Jewish community and thus a very high-profile individual in the town. Everyone in the community knew, therefore, that Jerzy Kluger was Jewish. He remembers the day when he and Karol learned that they had been admitted to secondary school. Thinking that he had the news first, Jerzy went to inform his friend. When he heard that young Lolek was at Mass, he went into the Catholic church for the first time to find him. As Jerzy entered, a woman who was leaving the church recognized him as a Jewish boy and snubbed him conspicuously. Noticing the incident, young Karol, who was about 10 years old at the time, comforted his friend, saying, "Aren't we both children of God?"

Jerzy spent many afternoons sitting in the kitchen next to the Wojtylas' coal stove listening to Lolek's father tell stories about his military career and stories out of history. In turn,

A young Karol Wojtyla (second row, left) is shown with fellow students of his school in Poland in this photograph from 1932.

Lolek went to the Klugers' 10-room apartment overlooking the town square and listened to music performed by a string quartet composed of two Jews and two Catholics.

With Jerzy, and with other Jewish and Catholic friends, Karol enjoyed sports of all kinds. When he wasn't playing soccer, he would take daring swims in the flooded Skawa River. Then, in the winter, he played ice hockey on the river's frozen surface and went skiing in the Tatras Mountains. "There wasn't much of a means to go up the mountain in those days, there was only one lift," Kluger remembers. "We used to walk three, four, five hours to get to the top and then ski down in seven minutes. We were like all the other mountain boys, winter was long in Poland." (Papal biographer George Weigel noted that throughout his life, John Paul was "a terrific sportsman. . . . As a young man he was a very active soccer player, a skier, a hiker. As a young priest he became very involved in a ministry to university students built around hiking, skiing, and kayaking.") However, an old Polish colleague of John Paul's once commented that he thought the pontiff's affinity for the mountains and mountain people went beyond his love for skiing or hiking. "He came from the foothills, not the mountains, but he *belongs* with the mountain people. He loves their songs and poetry; he shares their simplicity, their sense of humor, their independence, their love of freedom. The mountain people were never serfs, so they symbolize the equality that exists between man and man; they have always been in love with freedom. Karol Wojtyla has a lot of the mountain man in his make-up. He too is in love with freedom."

As much as he was an excellent athlete and outdoorsman, Karol was also a first-class student. Success in academics seemed to come easy to him: He was naturally gifted, brilliant, in fact. One of his teachers, a priest named Zacher, recalled him as "the nearest thing to a genius I ever had the good fortune to teach." Another who knew Karol well commented, "He was outstandingly clever, but he didn't keep it to himself. He used to go out of his way to help other boys who were a bit slow. He never grudged his time to them." An avid reader, Karol regularly borrowed books on a range of subjects from the local library and devoured them during long nights by the fire at his family home. This reading made his conversation fascinating. "He was a marvelous story-teller," remembers one old friend, "and conversation when he was around was always lively. He had such a wide knowledge of all sorts of things. You know, he'd throw in a bit of Homer, or a line from Virgil, but there was a lot of fun and gossip there too."

These things—physical and intellectual exertion, tempered and leavened by a pious reverence for God—made him happy and content. But this is not to say that he did not know sadness. Karol's mother died of heart and kidney problems when the boy was just one month short of his ninth birthday. Then, when he was 12, his 26-year-old brother Edmund, the physician, died of scarlet fever. Looking back, friends say Karol lost his childhood at age 12, when he lost his brother. Still, Karol's father was kind and loving as he was strict, and he did his best to make a good,

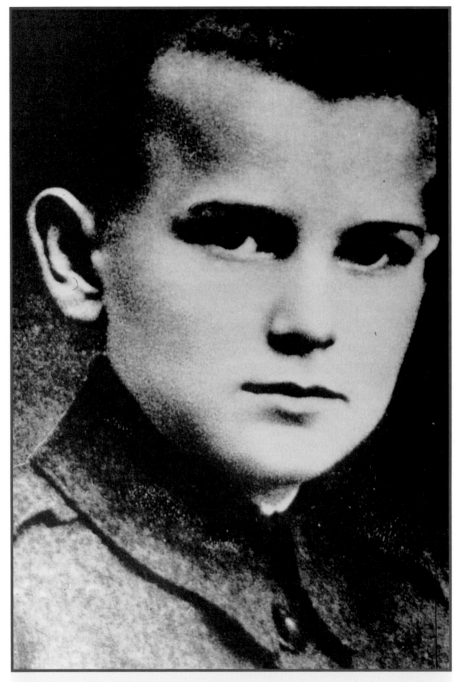

The future pope as a 12-year old student: Karol Wojtyla would become the first non-Italian pope since the sixteenth century.

if modest, home for his son. After his mother died, Karol and his father lived in a spartan, one-room apartment behind the Catholic church that in winter was quite chilly. Karol's father sewed his clothes and made sure the boy saw to his studies diligently. "He tried to develop the same discipline in his son that he instilled in his soldiers," Jerzy Kluger recalls. Still, father didn't forget about play. Kluger remembers entering the Wojtylas' apartment and finding father and son playing soccer with a ball made of rags.

As a young man, Wojtyla developed a passion for the arts, especially poetry and theater. As biographer Mary Craig wrote: "There was no school production in which he didn't take part, and it was usually the leading part. When the school drama group toured southeast Poland with a repertoire ranging from modern Polish drama to Shakespeare, he produced many of the plays himself. He was renowned not only for his acting but for his superb dancing, performing Strauss waltzes, folk dances and the difficult Polish mazurkas, polonaises and Krakowiaks with equal abandon and skill."

Wojtyla graduated from secondary school in 1938, after which he and his father moved to Krakow so that he could study literature and philosophy at Jagiellonian University. There, with Nazism on the rise in Europe, Wojtyla founded an underground theater company for which he wrote and acted in plays that frequently dealt with oppression. (Interestingly, when Wojtyla wrote his first three plays in 1939 and 1940, his heroes were all Jews drawn from the Bible: David, Job, and Jeremiah.) Wojtyla also participated in poetry readings and literary discussion groups. Contemporaries recall him as an intense and gifted actor and a fine singer. But they also recall him as a seriously devout young man. As he had in his old hometown, he continued to serve on the altar at Mass each morning; he also founded a Catholic religious society at his school.

After the Germans invaded Poland, all colleges, high schools, and seminaries were closed. Wojtyla escaped deportation and imprisonment in late 1940 by taking a job as a stonecutter in a quarry owned by a chemical plant, an industrial conglomerate thought vital to the Nazi war effort. A few months later, in February 1941, Wojtyla's 61-year-old father died. The pious old man had hoped to live long enough to see Wojtyla commit himself to the Catholic priesthood, but it would be another year and a half before Wojtyla would finally make this decision and begin studying at an underground seminary in Krakow. For the time being, he worked his grim job, acted in underground theater, and became active in the anti-Nazi resistance.

Wojtyla had not forgotten his Jewish friends. He joined UNIA, an underground organization of Catholic Poles specifically pledged to aid Jews in escaping the Holocaust. The UNIA provided false papers to some 50,000 Jews and hid approximately 2,500 Jewish children throughout the course of the occupation. UNIA also sponsored "cultural resistance," which involved upholding a vision of democracy, human rights, faith, and religious freedom. Wrote Mary Craig:

> Powerful forces were at work in the young Wojtyla. All around him he saw suffering and misery; men and women famished and reduced to the level of chattels; children snatched from their parents and deported; Jewish families brutally rounded up and sent God knew where; schools and universities closed down; and underneath the dogged determination of the Poles, the constant fear: fear for one's family and friends, fear for oneself; fear of the knock on the door in the middle of the night; of sudden arrest by the Gestapo. Nazi jackboots strutting around the city underlined the atmosphere of terror. The brutality he witnessed every day, the degrading conditions in which he and his fellow-laborers toiled, affected him with something close to despair.

It was in fact out of this despair that Wojtyla reached to grasp his faith- and life-affirming mission in the priesthood.

During the early days of the occupation, Wojtyla joined a lay religious discussion group headed by his friend Jan Tyranowski, a tailor more than twice his age. Early in their talks, the devout Tyranowski recommended that all in the group read and comment upon the writings of St. John of the Cross. This sixteenth-century Spanish mystic and poet had written of the *via negative*, the darkness in which the soul finds God. Wojtyla, amid the less abstract darkness of Europe's new Nazi medievalism, found not God (whom he'd known well along) but his calling to serve that God. Citing St. John of the Cross and the tailor Jan Tyranowski, the latter whom he recognized years later as "a true apostle of God's greatness," Wojtyla spoke to Archbishop Adam Stefan Sapieha of Krakow about his desire for the priesthood, and the archbishop accepted him as a student in the secret seminary he conducted, now that all seminaries were banned. As biographer Craig wrote: "[Wojtyla's] vocation had been born of the chaos and savagery of the Occupation, which had driven him to put his life at the service of others, to keep the flickering flame of humanity alive in such profound darkness."

"When Wojtyla entered the ranks of Sapieha's secret seminarians in October 1942," wrote Carl Bernstein and Marco Politi, "he found himself plugged in to a carefully organized system. Each student was assigned a professor who supervised him individually. Classes were held in convents, churches, and private houses. Students were instructed to keep their studies secret from acquaintances and to maintain outwardly secular routines." Thus, while studying by night, Wojtyla continued with his other activities as laborer, clandestine actor and student, and resistance member until August 1944, at which point he disappeared in a way that was neither miraculous nor remarkable, any more than it was accidental.

"One of the methods the Germans regularly used to terrorize the Poles was the *lapanka*, the practice of making a sudden swoop on a street, any street, cordoning it off, setting up road-blocks, and arresting or shooting all those who had

In 1943, Jews in Warsaw, Poland, are gathered up and marched away under a smoke filled sky. As part of German dictator Adolf Hitler's plan to take over the world, German SS troops invaded the city and set it afire. Under Nazi rule, Poles could be threatened, shot on the street at random, or rounded up and taken to concentration camps.

the misfortune to be there at the time," wrote Craig. "When Warsaw rose in revolt in August 1944, the Germans stepped up this practice throughout the rest of Poland, as a means of discouraging them from following suit." After a particularly brutal lapanka occurring in Krakow that August, from which young Wojtyla narrowly escaped with his life, Archbishop Sapieha decided to take his six underground students under his wing and hide them permanently in his residence, which some called the Archbishop's Palace, on Franciszkanska Street.

After one day of not showing up for work, the six were fully committed. Following their unauthorized absence, they simply had to remain indoors. Without jobs, they were wanted men: their names on the types of lists one didn't want one's name to be on. Wojtyla and his cohorts did not leave the grounds of the archbishop's residence for many months. The only exercise they got was a stroll or volleyball in the courtyard of the so-called palace. Here they remained until January 12, 1945, when the welcome, for the moment, Russian "liberators" finally swept through Poland after camping for months on the eastern side of the Vistula River.

In six years, the Germans had killed 6,300,000 Poles, 3 million of these being Jews. One-quarter of the entire Polish population had been wiped out. "Life is strange," an old priest would comment to a *Time* magazine reporter in the late 1970s. "They tried to wipe Poland off the face of the earth. Yet now Hitler is dead, the Nazis are no more, and the despised Poland has given a Pope to the world."

Once the war was over, Wojtyla returned to the reopened Jagiellonian University, where he completed his third- and fourth-year theology studies and soon found himself elected vice president of the student body. Supporting himself as a teaching assistant, he earned marks that placed him near the top of his class. Then on November 1, 1946, Archbishop Sapieha personally ordained Wojtyla a priest in the chapel of the "palace." Wojtyla said his first Mass one day later. And one day after that, his former coworkers from the quarry presented him with a cassock, one he took with him the following morning when he returned to Wadowice, there to say Mass in the parish of his childhood. A week after that, he administered a baptism for the first time, pouring water over the infant daughter of two old childhood friends. He wrote that he felt his life closing in a beautiful and preordained circle.

3

The Road to the Papacy

ALMOST IMMEDIATELY AFTER HIS ORDINATION, WOJTYLA WAS DISPATCHED to the Eternal City of Rome for postgraduate studies. "The year and a half he would spend in Italy was a most precious foundation for Wojtyla's career," wrote Tad Szulc. "His road to the papacy began at the Belgian College at No. 26, Via del Quirinale, a stone's throw from Palazzo Quirinale where Italian presidents reside, just before Christmas 1946." But Wojtyla only lived at Belgian College, a Jesuit establishment. He studied at the Angelicum University, not far away. Founded by the Dominicans in 1577, Angelicum was favored by Wojtyla's conservative superiors back in Krakow, who did not care for the liberal tradition embraced by the Jesuits and wanted to protect their young protégé from what they considered to be subversive in the church.

Many years later, shortly after his election to the throne of St. Peter, John Paul said, "How alive is in my memory my first

Karol Wojtyla appears in the back row, right, in this 1948 photo taken during his stay at Belgian College. The time the young priest spent in Italy had a great impact on his career.

encounter with the Eternal City. It was late autumn of 1946, when, after I was ordained a priest, I arrived here to continue my studies. . . . I carried in my eye the image of Rome from history, from literature and from the entire Christian tradition. For many days, I criss-crossed the city, which then had one million inhabitants, and I couldn't fully find the image of that Rome I had brought with me. Slowly, slowly, I found it. It came to me especially after touring the catacombs—the Rome of the beginnings of Christianity, the Rome of the Apostles, the Rome of Martyrs, the Rome that exists at the beginnings of the Church and, at the same time, of the great culture that we inherit."

Early in his tenure at Rome, young Wojtyla had the privilege of meeting Pope Pius XII, during a brief private audience for seminarians held in the same Apostolic Palace where John Paul would one day live, work, and die. Later on, shortly after Easter of 1947, Wojtyla drove to San Giovanni Rotondo, near Naples, to attend Mass and meet the famous Father Fancesco Forgione Pio, an old monk and worker of miracles whose stigmata wounds on his hands, feet, and sides were legendary. (It is rumored that Pio took young Wojtyla by the hand and advised him he would one day head the church. Years later, John Paul II presided over the beatification of "Padre Pio.")

Wojtyla passed summa cum laude the exams for his seminary teaching certificate, the equivalent of a master's degree, on July 3, 1947. Then he remained in Rome for another year, cobbling away at a lengthy dissertation in which he considered influences derived from St. Francis of Assisi by St. John of the Cross. Although this project, a massive and complex one, received praise and the highest possible grades from Wojtyla's proctor, the young priest was nevertheless denied a doctorate in sacred theology over a technicality. Under the Angelicum's rules, dissertations had to be published before a doctorate would be awarded, and the impoverished Karol Wojtyla simply did not have the money to pay a printer. After absorbing this blow, on June 15, 1948, Wojtyla departed Rome for his native Poland, a land rapidly slipping behind the dark shadow of the Soviet Iron Curtain.

As Wojtyla returned home, the Polish Catholic Church was undergoing major changes. Cardinal August Hlond, the primate of Poland, died on October 23, 1948. Two weeks later, Pope Pius XII named 47-year-old Bishop Stefan Wyszynski to succeed Hlond in that post and as archbishop of Gniezno and Warsaw.

Wojtyla had great admiration for Wyszynski, a socially conscious scholar, politician, anti-Communist, anti-Nazi, and advocate for a "Third Way" between liberalism and Marxism. During World War II, Wyszynski had lived in hiding because of his anti-Nazi writings before the invasion of Poland and also to facilitate his growing links with the military underground. Throughout much of the war, Wyszynski was active in the resistance: serving as chaplain with armed Polish freedom fighters in Polish forests and as professor at a secret university in Warsaw. Although an anti-Communist, Wyszynski was equally skeptical of capitalism, which he saw as having its own excesses. In tone and spirit and message, Wojtyla was to learn much from Wyszynski over time. (In 1946, the young Wyszynski [just 45] was appointed bishop of Lublin, the seat of the Catholic University.)

One of Wojtyla's first assignments in Poland was to serve as vicar in the poor rural parish of Niegowic, approximately 30 miles to the east of Krakow. The parish was one of the oldest in Poland, founded in 1049, but was nevertheless something of an ecclesiastic backwater embracing 13 shabby villages on both sides of the Raba River. Wojtyla and another vicar worked under the longtime parish priest, who had been in the post nearly 50 years. Most of Wojtyla's time was spent in the way of a visiting ministry, making annual visits to shut-ins across the large, rural parish. "You go out in your cassock," he told a friend, "your overcoat, your alb and biretta over beaten path in the snow. But snow will cling to your cassock, then it will thaw out indoors, and freeze again outside, forming a heavy bell around your legs, which gets heavier and heavier, preventing you from taking long strides. By evening, you [can] hardly drag your legs. But you have to go on, because you know that people wait for you, that they wait all year for this meeting. . . ." At the same time that he tended these duties, Wojtyla attended Jagiellonian University, where, armed with his old dissertation from Rome, he quickly received both a master's and a doctorate in sacred theology.

The spring of 1949 found Wojtyla recalled to Krakow and assigned by his old friend Cardinal Sapieha to the post of vicar at St. Florian's Church. There he developed close contacts with intellectuals, artists, and students, many of them affiliated with the nearby Faculty of Fine Arts and the new Polytechnic (engineering faculty) at Jagiellonian. The popular Father Wojtyla wove about himself at St. Florian's an ever-growing network of friends and acquaintances that, in time, became known as the Wojtyla milieu, a group that would remain quite close, cohesive, and active even after his elevation to the papacy. As Tad Szulc reported: "Wojtyla performed regular parish church duties along with his work with university students, which ranged from special sermons and homilies to lectures and discussions in St. Florian's sacristy and visits to students' dormitories and rabbit-warren apartments for late-night bull sessions. He took students to the theater and the movies, played chess with them, and led them on mountain hikes."

Wojtyla's longtime patron, Cardinal Sapieha, passed away on July 23, 1951, at the age of 85. Subsequently, Sapieha's replacement ordered Wojtyla to take a two-year leave of absence to study for still another doctorate. Now, in addition to furthering his studies, Wojtyla also had extended time to himself for the writing of poetry, essays, dramas, and whatever else struck his fancy. But all around him, as he studied and wrote, dark forces were gathering. In January 1951, Bishop Czeslaw Kaczmarek of Kielce, a diocese in south-central Poland, was arrested on vague charges of treason and espionage. Held for two years prior to trial, he was then found guilty on all counts and sentenced to 12 years of hard labor. The arrest marked a turning point, a new and unprecedented round of intimidation and persecution directed against the church by the officially atheist Polish Communist government, which feared the church as a breeding ground for revolution and nationalism. The years that followed would be characterized by selective arrests of senior prelates.

Under pressure from Communist officials, the administration of Jagiellonian University closed the school's theology department during 1954. Shortly thereafter, Jagiellonian's ecumenical theology staff quietly reconvened with their students at the Seminary of Krakow, under the auspices of the Archdiocese of Krakow. In this furtive atmosphere, Wojtyla continued his studies. At the same time, he was hired as a non-tenured professor by the Catholic University of Lublin. He commuted daily between Lublin and Krakow on an overnight train, getting what sleep he could during the journey. Wojtyla played the role of teacher in one city and student in the other. As if that were not enough to occupy him, he at the same time founded a Catholic marriage counseling service that *Time* would eventually describe as "perhaps the most successful marriage institute in Christianity."

During 1956, Wojtyla received an appointment to a tenure-track chair of ethics at Catholic University. Two years later, he was made auxiliary bishop of Krakow. Characteristically, Wojtyla was off in the woods when he received this news; he was on an outdoors adventure with students, kayaking and camping near the Lyna River in the lake region of northern Poland, merging his woodlands sojourn with a visit to a famous sanctuary dedicated to the cult of the Virgin Mary. Students remember him on that trip, relaxed and happy amid the mountains, lakes, and rivers, carrying a typed manuscript for his new book, a study of the family called *Love and Responsibility*, which he doled out to them chapter by chapter for reading and discussion by fireside every evening. It was on August 18, three days after the Feast of the Assumption, that he was called to the telephone in the nearby rectory and advised that Pope Pius XII, destined to die just two months later, had appointed him auxiliary bishop.

Pius's successor, John XXIII, unveiled his plans for the Second Vatican Council on January 25, 1959. Three years later, when the council began in earnest the deliberations that would revolutionize the church, the 42-year-old bishop from Krakow

Father Wojtyla surrounded himself with artists, intellectuals, and students. His ability to connect with people is the reason many credit him with humanizing the papacy.

was one of the most eloquent participants. The new pope called the process of the Second Vatican Council *aggiornamento*, the Italian word meaning "to bring up-to-date." Pope John's greatest wish was that the council would restore Christian unity in an ecumenical spirit, move toward ending differences between bickering Christian churches, promote religious liberty across the globe, and in this way make the church reborn. Bishop Karol Wojtyla entered into the process enthusiastically. That same year, Pope John named him acting archbishop of Krakow.

As archbishop, Wojtyla dealt pragmatically with Poland's Communist rulers, accommodating them just enough that they thought him, wrongly, to be an improvement over previous Catholic hard-line leaders who had staunchly opposed their philosophy. Wojtyla's May 29, 1967, appointment as cardinal by Pope Paul VI, the pope installed after the 1963 death of Pope John XXIII, was welcomed by the officially atheist Polish government. Through the late 1960s and early 1970s, Wojtyla engaged in a complex strategy that honored Catholic beliefs and traditions while at the same time placated the Communist government on what he believed to be trivial fronts. As Mary Craig noted, Wojtyla's top priority "was to find novel ways of spreading the faith, encouraging worship and religious teaching, and to create a powerful [Church] structure in Krakow. At the same time, he spared no effort to make the archdiocese a major intellectual and cultural center. There was nothing like it in Poland. This had to be done, however, against the background of continuing pressures by the regime against the Polish Church. In the contest with the Communist authorities over the rights of the Church and the faithful, Wojtyla sought to avoid open conflict. But while he preferred—whenever possible—to achieve his objectives by negotiation and even selective compromise, he never abandoned his principles nor ceded on the essentials. His strategy was to wear down the Communists with personal or written protests over any violation of what he considered to be Church

Pope Paul VI places the cardinal's hat on Karol Wojtyla, declaring him the Archbishop of Krakow, Poland, on May 29, 1967. The archbishop was such a skilled diplomat that he even appealed to Poland's atheistic government.

rights, or human rights in general, including the freedom of Catholic education and catechism."

As Wojtyla knew, Polish nationalist (and, therefore, anti-communism) feeling was deeply linked with the Poles' devout affinity for their church. Like the Poles' love of their land and heritage, their devotion to Catholicism was heartfelt and complete, just as their allegiance to the authority of the current state was purely cynical and forced. In synch with these realities, Karol proved himself always to be a calculating, pragmatic, and effective enemy of communism. He was, as one observer noted, "a powerful preacher and sophisticated intellectual able to defeat Marxists in their own line of dialogue."

His art lay in subtle negotiation. He routinely cooperated with the Communist authorities on a host of small and trivial matters, having made the decision to choose his battles wisely. But in return for not being a nagging thorn in the side of the government, Wojtyla insisted on permission to build new churches, start youth groups, and ordain as many priests as he would like without fear of punishment. (When asked if he feared retaliation from the government, Wojtyla responded: "I'm not afraid of them. They are afraid of me." He told a friend that he had "the people of Poland and God—not necessarily in that order—on his side.")

Throughout all this, Wojtyla remained energetically intellectual, writing numerous books. His *Love and Responsibility* (1960) proved a vital mediation on marriage and the family. Translated into dozens of languages, the book eventually became an influential bestseller around the world. Throughout the text, Wojtyla argued for the inherent equality of man and woman in marriage while also scrutinizing sexual psychopathology as it related to and derived from theology. About this same time, he composed a companion work—a play that was part meditative essay and part drama. Published under the pseudonym Andrzej Jawien, *In Front of the Jeweler's Shop* looked at the sacrament of marriage through the prism of inspirational, mystical, and sometimes surprisingly sensual language. However, in both the book and the play, Wojtyla adhered to an almost-medieval model for marital relations, one that circumscribed contraception. Thus his approach was one that many modern readers found contrary and alien.

Wojtyla's second doctoral thesis, *Evaluation of the Possibility of Constructing a Christian Ethic Based on the System of Max Scheler*, saw print the same year as *Love and Responsibility*. The year 1969 marked the publication of his next major treatise. *The Acting Person* constituted Wojtyla's in-depth consideration of phenomenology, a theme he lectured on during a 1978 visit to the United States.

Complexity defined him. Two years previous to his U.S. trip, when Wojtyla was invited to lead spiritual exercises before a visibly ailing Pope Paul VI at a Lenten retreat, his first three references were to the Bible, St. Augustine, and German

Cardinal Karol Wojtyla greets the crowd from Krakow's Wawel Cathedral on July 9, 1967. A decade later, he would be greeting crowds from the Vatican balcony.

philosopher Martin Heidegger. One year after that, Wojtyla gave a talk in Milan on the topic "The Problem of Creating Culture through Human Praxis." His reputation, among churchmen at least, was now international. His fellow cardinals recognized him as one of the more thoughtful and scholarly of their number, not to mention the most strategic and calculating, as documented in his seemingly endless chess game with the Communist rulers of Poland. Not all who knew Wojtyla presumed to understand him completely, but all agreed he seemed destined for something special.

4

The Polish Pope

ALTHOUGH HE HAD ESTABLISHED HIMSELF AS A HIGHLY RESPECTED intellectual and philosopher of the church—as well as a man skilled in such practicalities as fundraising and administration—nobody expected that the Sacred College of Cardinals would choose Wojtyla as the next pope after the sudden and unexpected death of John Paul I. The recently deceased John Paul I had reigned only briefly after the death of Pope Paul VI, who himself died in September 1978 after only a few weeks in the papacy.

Nevertheless, when the cardinals were unable to agree on a candidate after seven rounds of balloting, Wojtyla was chosen as a compromise candidate in the eighth round, late in the afternoon of October 16.

Thus he became the first non-Italian pope in 455 years (the last had been Adrian VI, who held the position from 1522 to 1523).

THE ART OF PAPAL SELECTION

The "conclave" in which the pope is chosen is a gathering of the College of Cardinals—men of cardinal rank from all around the globe. Sequestered inside the ornate confines of the Vatican's Sistine Chapel, with only a few helpers to tend to them, these men choose the next pope from among their own number. The word *conclave* actually means "under lock and key," from the Latin words *cum clavi*. To assure the secrecy of the gathering, the cardinals are locked within the chapel, and all means of communication with the outside world are cut off, except for messengers who can take the most necessary communications in and out, along with foods and medicines as needed.

"According to the reforms instituted by Pope Paul VI, only cardinals under age 80 years of age can vote for a Pope," wrote Thomas J. Reese, SJ, in an article appearing in the Jesuit magazine *America*. While setting the maximum number of voting cardinals at 120, Paul had also stipulated that no cardinal under 80 could be excluded.

There are three ways in which an election can take place, according to the constitution Romano Pontifici Eligendo. The first, which seldom happens, is when the cardinals, "as it were through the inspiration of the Holy Spirit, freely and spontaneously, unanimously and aloud, proclaim one individual as supreme pontiff." In other words, it arrives through a direct message from God. The cardinals must unanimously accept this form of election. The second method is by delegation, when the cardinal electors give the responsibility of the selection to a group of their members, made up of an odd number of nine or fewer cardinals.

The third and most common manner of electing the pope is by "scrutiny"—the name coming from the "scrutineers" who count the ballots. Great care is taken to avoid any sort of fraud or rigging of the ballots. "Three scrutineers are chosen by lot from among the electors with the least senior cardinal deacon drawing the names," explains Reese in the magazine *America*.

After the sudden death of Pope John Paul I, cardinals once again held a con-clave to elect a new pope. On October 14, 1978, cardinals enter the Sistine Chapel singing, following a mass in St. Peter's Church.

"He draws three additional names of cardinals (Infirmari) who will collect the ballots of any cardinals in the conclave who are too sick to come to the Sistine Chapel. A final three names are drawn by lot to act as revisers who review the work done by the scrutineers." Up until the election of John Paul II, the most favored process was secret popular vote. After his election, John Paul II eliminated the first two methods of choosing a pope. Thus, all popes going forward will—like John Paul II himself —be selected by popular, secret vote, unless a successor pope chooses to revise the rules yet again.

The papal election is not at all like a presidential election. It's considered improper for cardinals to lobby or campaign among their colleagues for the job of pope. Theoretically, the cardinals' votes are supposed to be driven by God's will, uninfluenced by practical concerns of the material world. In reality, however, there is a very necessary and very conscious element of practicality that enters into the equation. There are certain skills that a pope simply must have, that not all cardinals have. For starters, a pope doesn't need to be Italian, but he does need to be fluent in the Italian language to be able to direct the Vatican's vast bureaucracy, which operates in that language. What's more, a pope must have a demonstrated skill at managing a large enterprise, which the Vatican certainly is. Thus, non–Italian speaking cardinals from tiny, remote outposts of Catholicism are rarely considered viable prospects for pope.

Votes are cast, with two rounds of balloting in the mornings and two in the afternoons. After each vote, the ballots are burned in a small stove within the Sistine Chapel. The natural fire sends black smoke wafting out of the chimney, indicating to the world outside that no pope has yet been chosen. This goes on until one of the cardinals earns a two-thirds-plus-one majority among his peers. When that finally happens, chemicals are added to the fire to turn the smoke white, thus telling the world the happy news. After his election, John Paul II decreed that upon the election of future popes, the bells of the Sistine Chapel should be rung. This order derived from the fact that with Wojtyla's election in 1978, the smoke rising from the chimney appeared to be neither black nor white, thus creating brief confusion in the crowd. John Paul also decreed that cardinals need not remain locked within the Sistine Chapel for the entire time of the conclave, and should instead be assigned comfortable sleeping accommodations within the Vatican.

The cardinals use ballots bearing the printed Latin words *Eligio in Summum Pontificem,* meaning: "I elect as Supreme Pontiff." When the cardinals write the name of their preferred candidate, they are supposed to try to disguise their handwriting in order to insure anonymity in balloting. Following this, the cardinals fold their ballots twice, and then wait their turn to carry their individual ballots up to the altar. Arriving at the alter, each man announces loudly: "I call as my witness Christ the Lord who will be my judge that my vote is given to the one who before God I think should be elected." After all the cardinals have cast their ballots, the box containing them is shaken and opened, and the ballots are counted before all. With the results of the balloting made instantly available to the cardinals, they can see which candidates are developing into "favorites," and which are lost causes, and can adjust their future votes accordingly. In this way, a consensus is eventually reached.

After three days with no clear winner, the cardinals normally take a day off to pray, mediate, and speak among themselves—often organizing into blocks of votes, and orchestrating an outcome. After another three days, there will, if necessary, be yet another break. In the unlikely event that 30 votes slip by without any one of the men receiving a sold two-thirds-plus-one majority, then the election process is altered. At that point, a simple majority may become enough to elect a pope, provided that a simple majority also agrees to this suspension of the standard two-thirds-plus-one rule.

Here is an interesting and, some might think, ironic, detail about the process of papal election that not many people realize: Although only the college of cardinals can elect a pope, the new pontiff actually need not be from among their numbers. The College of Cardinals has the power to elect any Catholic male—such as a simple priest, or even a married Catholic layman—as Supreme Pontiff. However, by long tradition, the cardinals always choose among themselves.

Following the final election of the pope, various helpers (including the secretary of the conclave, the master of ceremonies, and his assistants) receive a summons to appear before the cardinals and stand as witnesses to what will take place next. The dean of the College of Cardinals asks the following question of the winner of the election, "Do you accept your canonical

"WITH OBEDIENCE IN FAITH TO CHRIST, MY LORD, AND WITH TRUST IN THE MOTHER OF CHRIST AND THE CHURCH, IN SPITE OF GREAT DIFFICULTIES, I ACCEPT."

—Pope John Paul II,
accepting his election as pope in 1978

election as supreme pontiff?" After the new pope says "yes," the dean asks him what name he wishes to go by.

Once these formalities are accomplished, the new pope enters the sacristy where, helped by two cardinals, he dresses in full papal regalia. These include the pope's traditional white cassock, white stockings, and red slippers; the latter embroidered with gold crosses. Then, re-entering the Sistine Chapel, he sits on the papal throne for the first time and has the Ring of the Fisherman placed on his finger. After this, one by one, the members of the College of Cardinals advance, kiss the new pope's hand, and kneel before him. By tradition, three days after his election, the pope will say his first papal Mass in St. Peter's Basilica that lies directly above Peter's tomb. On the same day, shortly after that mass, he will be crowned with the crown of the supreme pontiff.

POPE JOHN PAUL II

Karol Wojtyla garnered 97 votes on the eighth ballot of the conclave in October 1978. At this, the College of Cardinals erupted into applause for the archbishop of Krakow, who sat with tears in his eyes. Once the applause had died away and Wojtyla had composed himself, Cardinal Villot asked him: "Do you, most reverend Lord Cardinal, accept your election as Supreme Pontiff, which has been canonically carried out?" Wojtyla

Pope John Paul II greets a cheering crowd from the balcony of St. Peter's Basilica on October 16, 1978.

nodded. Then he answered: "With obedience in faith to Christ, my lord, and with trust in the mother of Christ and the church, in spite of great difficulties, I accept." After this, he announced his new name: *John Paul II.*

Shortly thereafter, Cardinal Angelo Felici addressed the crowd in St. Peter's Square and announced the papal selection: Cardinal Wojtyla of Poland. The unfamiliar name of a non-Italian cardinal caused stunned silence; it lasted only a moment, however, and then gave way to loud, enthusiastic applause. Soon the Roman Catholic Church's first Slavic pope stood before the faithful. "All honor to Jesus Christ," he announced in Italian. Then: "Dear brothers and sisters: We are still grieved after the death of our most beloved John Paul I. And now the most eminent cardinals have called a new bishop of Rome from a far-off land; far yet so near through the communion of faith and in the Christian tradition…" Then, smiling out of modesty, he added: "I don't know if I express myself in your… our… Italian language well enough. If I make a mistake, you will correct me." Now more applause came—loud, fervent, prolonged—along with the realization that the new Polish pope had already won the hearts of Romans and the world.

South Africa's Cardinal Owen McCann, interviewed the next day, had only good things to say about the newly named pope. "I think he is going to be a fine Pope," McCann predicted. "I think he is a very spiritual man, and most certainly is pastorally minded."

In addition to being the first non-Italian pope in centuries, Wojtyla was also, at 58, the youngest Pope in 132 years. "I was afraid to receive this nomination," he told the crowd from the balcony, "but I did it in the spirit of obedience to our Lord and in the total confidence in his mother, the most holy Madonna."

Friends were astonished. Jerzy Kluger, then a businessman in Rome, whooped and cheered. Danuta Michalowska, an actress friend who had performed with Wojtyla in his underground drama group during the Nazi occupation, sent him a formal message of congratulation in which she lamented that they could no longer stay in touch because of his new eminence. One week later, in a handwritten note, John Paul assured her he could never and would never live without the friendships that had been among God's greatest gift to him. Another friend—the Rev. Father Tadeusz Styczen (pronounced Stee-chen), a Polish priest and philosopher who succeeded to Wojtyla 's chair at the University of Lublin—received assurances that they would continue their annual hikes in the Carpathians, and a polite inquiry as to his skills and willingness to help a novice pope shape encyclicals.

On the first day of his pontificate, John Paul II went to a hospital in Rome to visit an ailing Bishop who was an old friend. "A crowd gathered in the clinic's corridors for a glimpse of him," wrote Tad Szulc, "but the Pope had to be reminded that they expected a blessing. Smiling sheepishly, he made the sign of the cross, remarking, 'I'm not used to it yet.' ..." Later that same day, the pope entertained Polish friends at an informal reception. Jerzy Kluger and his British wife held a place of honor. Then, during the long evening that followed, John Paul gave orders that his cardinal's red skullcap be placed at the altar of the Polish Virgin in Vilnius, the capital city of Soviet Lithuania—even though it would have to be smuggled there. One of John Paul II's biographers notes that when his election was announced, Yuri Andropov, leader of the Soviet Union's KGB intelligence agency, warned the Soviet Politburo that they would face trouble ahead with this pope: he was the first to emerge from a Soviet dominated state, and a great Polish nationalist. Andropov could not have been more correct.

At the same time that he made symbolic gestures against communism, however, John Paul signaled that he intended, in effect, to restore the old monarchic and absolute model of the papacy—effectively abandoning the canons of collegiality and compromise that had been the hallmark of the Second Vatican Council. The smiling, self-effacing, convivial Pope John Paul II was soon to show the world that underneath his charm lurked an unbending doctrinal authoritarian. Soon theological dissent within the Catholic Church would be banned with the same shrillness that political dissent was banned in the Soviet bloc. But John Paul saw no equivalence. While what he once called the "illusory power" of Soviet leaders flowed only from man, the "true authority"—as he described it—of the pope flowed from God. And John Paul intended to use his "true authority" to fight not only communism, but all other aspects of modernity, including sexual liberation and moves to liberalize the church.

"Fear not to receive Christ and to accept his Authority," the pope said in his Inauguration Day sermon. "Fear Not! ...

Open wide the doors to Christ and His authority of salvation! Open the frontiers of states, [of] economic and political systems, of broad domains of culture [and] civilization [and] development! Fear not! Christ knows what lives within man.… Only He knows!" In every aspect, John Paul saw the works and strictures of man as temporal and unimportant as compared to the works and laws of God. Going forward he would aim his rhetoric and actions against the liberal sexual ethics of the West and reform voices within the church, just as surely as he would aim them against Soviet domination of Eastern Europe. While the latter theater of operations would prove supremely successful for the pope, the former would not. Indeed, John Paul's conservatism would, in the end, cost him prestige in Rome and abroad, and cost his church millions of members.

5

Bringing an End to Communism

EDWARD GIEREK, THE FIRST SECRETARY OF THE PZPR—THE POLISH Communist Party—and therefore the secular leader of Poland, approached Cardinal Wojtyla's elevation to the papacy warily. One day after the election, Gierek, along with Poland's largely honorary president, Henryk Jablonski, and Prime Minister Piotr Jaroszewicz, sent the new pope congratulations via telegram: "For the first time in ages, a son of the Polish nation—which is building the greatness and prosperity in its Socialist motherland in the unity and collaboration of all its citizens—sits in the Papal throne . . . [the son] of a nation known throughout the world for its special love and peace and for its warmest attachment to the cooperation and friendship of all peoples . . . a nation, which has made universally recognized contributions to human culture. . . . We express our conviction that these great causes will be served by the further development of relations between the Polish People's Republic and the Apostolic Capital."

Pope John Paul II became known for kissing the ground upon his arrival in a new nation. This photograph was taken on November 15, 1980, at Cologne-Bonn Airport in Germany.

Exactly nine months after leaving Warsaw as Cardinal Wojtyla, Pope John Paul II returned to Poland on June 1, 1979, to spend nine days. The image of him kissing the ground as he emerged from his airplane is a lasting one and the symbol of a gesture he would repeat again and again in his travels through the coming years to countries other than his native land. In Poland, huge, adoring crowds met the pope wherever he went: their sheer mass represented a great source of embarrassment for the Communist government. The pope added to his host's discomfort by reminding his fellow Poles of their human rights. "His secretary told me that was the great moment," said

Robert Moynihan, editor and publisher of the magazine *Inside the Vatican*. "There was a crowd of one million people, and he told them 'You are men. You have dignity. Don't crawl on your bellies.' It was the beginning of the end of the Soviet Union."

Leaders in Soviet Russia had feared that the pope's message would be along these lines and had urged the Communist leadership of Poland to deny the pope entry, but to no avail. As Gierek recalled: "[Leonid] Brezhnev said that he had heard that the [Polish] Church had invited the Pope to Poland. 'What do you say to that?' he asked me. I answered: 'We shall receive him with dignity.' Brezhnev said, 'I advise you not to receive him because it will cause you much trouble.' I replied: 'How can I not receive the Polish Pope since the majority of our compatriots are of Catholic faith, and for them the election was a great feast. Besides, what do you imagine I can tell the people? What are we closing the barrier to him?' Brezhnev said: 'Tell the Pope—he is a wise man—that he could announce publicly that he cannot come because he has been taken ill.' I answered: 'Comrade Leonid, I cannot do that. I must receive John Paul II.' Then I heard this [from Brezhnev]: '[Wladyslaw] Gomulka [Gierek's predecessor] was a better Communist because he would not receive Paul VI in Poland, and nothing terrible has happened. The Poles have already survived one such refusal, so they will survive it again if you do not let this Pope in.' I stated that 'political sense, however, dictates to me the necessity of letting him in.' Brezhnev said, 'So do what you want, so long as you and your Party do not regret it later'—and he terminated the conversation."

During John Paul's sojourn in his homeland, at least 9 million (out of 35 million) Poles saw him in person in the numerous cities, villages, and religious sites where he appeared. The pope also showed up on Poland's state-managed television. (Cameramen found themselves with orders to zoom in for tight shots of the pontiff, thus not to emphasize the throngs that followed him everywhere.)

On May 13, 1981, as Pope John Paul II rode through a crowd in St. Peter's Square, a Turkish citizen named Mehmet Ali Agca pulled a gun and shot the pope. The drawn weapon can be seen in the left of the photograph. Another assassination attempt took place one year later. Thereafter, the pope rode in a protected vehicle, affectionately referred to as the "popemobile."

The pope, honoring a promise made during negotiations with Polish authorities before his journey, made a point of arriving too late to participate in the May commemorations of the 900th anniversary of the martyrdom of St. Stanislaw. (The patron saint of Poland, St. Stanislaw is not only a revered saint of the church but a nationalist hero as well.) Nevertheless, the pope made a point of invoking St. Stanislaw's politically loaded name whenever possible throughout his tour of Polish towns and cities. As John Paul was well aware, religion and patriotism had always walked hand in hand in Poland, and the patriotism to which the church was attached was not a patriotism to the modern Socialist state, but to the eternal and spiritual Poland of ancient history and memory. Thus many of John Paul's homilies during his tour were less religious exhortations than they were complex treatises on Polish history and culture. "Thus," wrote Tad Szulc, "John Paul II had come back to Poland as preacher and teacher, historian and patriot, philosopher and theologian."

John Paul's visit set off alarm bells in Moscow. Within months, the Central Committee of the Soviet Communist Party approved a six-point "Decision to Work Against the Policies of the Vatican in Relation with Socialist States." Drafted and signed in November 1979, the decision called for the "mobilization" of the Communist parties in eastern bloc nations, the TASS Soviet state news agency, the Academy of Sciences, "and other organizations of the Soviet State" to launch "propaganda against the policies of the Vatican." Specifically, the KGB was instructed to demonstrate that "the leadership of the new Pope, John Paul II, is dangerous to the Catholic Church." As well, the Soviet Academy of Sciences was instructed to "improve the study of scientific atheism." The decision went on to claim: "The problem now is that . . . they [the Vatican] now use religion in the ideological struggle against Socialist lands . . . through new methods [they] try to increase religious fanaticism against the political and ideological principles of the Socialist societies. The Vatican, above all, applies this new propaganda, which constitutes a new policy."

Lech Walesa's Polish Independent Syndicate Solidarnosc (Solidarity Union) would coalesce shortly and begin its decade-long, and ultimately successful, struggle for Polish democracy. Years later, Walesa himself claimed John Paul's 1979 visit as the inspiration that started it all. "[Without John Paul II] there would be no end of Communism or at least [it would have happened] much later, and the end would have been bloody," Walesa said years later. During a historic Mass conducted at Victory Square in Warsaw on June 2, 1979, the pope insisted:

"It is not possible to understand the history of the Polish nation without Christ." Less than two years later, John Paul received in audience a delegation headed by Lech Walesa and his fellow unionists. "The Pope started this chain of events that led to the end of Communism," Walesa noted. "Before his Pontificate, the world was divided into blocs. Nobody knew how to get rid of Communism. He simply said: 'Don't be afraid, change the image of this land.'"

The historian Timothy Garton Ash takes things one step further: "Without the Pope, no Solidarity. Without Solidarity, no Gorbachev. Without Gorbachev, no fall of Communism." Even Mikhail Gorbachev himself, the last leader of the Soviet Union, eventually acknowledged the key role John Paul II played in the fall of Communism. "What has happened in Eastern Europe in recent years," he told a journalist in March 1992, "would not have been possible without the presence of this Pope, without the great role . . . that he has played on the world scene."

Washington Post columnist Anne Applebaum elaborates further:

> [T]his Pope . . . made an impact thanks to his unusual ability—derived from charisma and celebrity as well as faith—to get people out on the streets. As Natan Sharansky and others have written, Communist regimes achieved their greatest successes when they were able to atomize people, to keep them apart and keep them afraid. But when the pope first visited Poland in 1979, he was greeted not by a handful of little old ladies, as the country's leaders predicted, but by millions of people of all ages. My husband, 16 years old at the time, remembers climbing a tree on the outskirts of an airfield near Gniezno where the Pope was saying Mass and seeing an endless crowd, 'three kilometers in every direction.' The regime—its leaders, its police—were nowhere visible: 'There were so many of us, and so few of them.' That was also

Polish Solidarity leader Lech Walesa kisses the hand of Pope John Paul II on June 8, 1981. The pope's support of Solidarity is believed to be the reason for the first attempt on his life.

the trip in which the Pope kept repeating, 'Don't be afraid.' It wasn't a coincidence that Poles found the courage, a year later, to organize Solidarity, the first mass anticommunist political movement. It wasn't a coincidence that 'civil society' began to organize itself in other communist countries as well: If it could happen in Poland, it could happen in Hungary or East Germany.

In 1981, Poland's Communist authorities, responding to orders from Moscow, declared a state of emergency, arrested Walesa and other leaders of Solidarity, and banned the union. After this, Solidarity went underground and, if anything, became even more powerful, even more potent, even more of a threat to the Communist machine. During 1985, the rise of the reformer Mikhail Gorbachev to chairman of the Supreme Soviet and president of Russia ushered in a period of intense and vital political and economic reforms throughout the Soviet bloc. Almost immediately, Gorbachev abandoned the Brezhnev Doctrine, Soviet Russia's longstanding rule of intervening militarily to preserve Communist rule in satellite countries. In marked contrast, he instead encouraged the local Communist leaders to seek new ways of earning favor with the populations they'd previously governed with an iron fist. Thus, in 1989, Hungary's Communist government made constitutional changes that led to the creation of a multiparty system. During that same year, Communist dictators in Poland entered into extensive, formal talks with Solidarity, now once again legal and operating in sunlight. Free and open elections followed, which brought Solidarity to power as Poland's ruling party. They were the first non-Communist rulers of a Soviet satellite since 1948. Inspired by all this, East Germans began to rebel during the summer and fall of 1989. In step with his previous rejection of the Brezhnev Doctrine, Gorbachev refused to send troops to prop up the government of East German Communist leader Erich Honecker. Czechs and Slovaks in Czechoslovakia in turn demanded reforms, emancipation, and freedom. Among those spearheading the agitation in Prague was playwright and advocate-for-democracy Vaclav Havel, co-founder of the reform group Charter 77. In short order, the Communist Party of Czechoslovakia—humiliated and defeated on the public relations front—transferred power to Havel and his fellow reformers. The transfer was so quiet and without violence that journalists later labeled it the "Velvet Revolution." In striking contrast, Romania saw the violent and bloody overthrow of Communist hardliner Nicolae Ceausescu during December of that same fateful year. Ceausescu's fall was followed in rapid succession by the fall of the Communist parties in Bulgaria and Albania. Next, revolt spread to the heart of world communism: the Soviet Union. After weathering an attempted overthrow by Communist hardliners in 1991, Gorbachev was eventually obliged to pass power to Boris Yeltsin, who in turn made it his business to orchestrate the orderly shutdown of the Soviet Union. In this way the collapse of the Soviet network states came about, and in this way the Cold War between the West's free market states and the Soviet bloc reached its end.

Of course, other players besides the pope, most notably United States President Ronald Reagan, played important parts in the diplomacy and exercises in what eventually brought down the infrastructure of Soviet Communism. However, John Paul's role was at least key and at best essential to the final result.

In his 1994 book, *Crossing the Threshold of Hope*, John Paul II provided his own answer to the question most often posed to him regarding the death of Communism. The pope referred to the three young Portuguese children from Fatima who, upon the appearance of the Virgin Mary before them during the First World War, heard the phrase "Russia will convert." John Paul wrote that the three "could not have invented those predictions. They did not know the history or the geography, and even less were they familiar with social movements and ideological developments." Indeed, the revolution that brought the Communists to power in Russia had not yet even occurred. "And nevertheless it happened as they had announced." He saw himself, therefore, as nothing but a cog in the wheel of a divine plan: a man placed by God at a certain point of history, with certain God-bequeathed principles and instincts, meant to do a particular job. But John Paul also added that "in a certain sense Communism as a system fell by itself . . . as a consequence of its own errors and abuse."

Pope John Paul II greets former leader of the Soviet Union Mikhail Gorbachev at the Vatican on November 18, 1996. Gorbachev gave the anti-Communist pope partial credit for the collapse of the Iron Curtain.

Characteristically, in negotiating with the last leader of Soviet Russia, John Paul at the same time made a friend. In the years after the Soviet Union ceased to be, Mikhail Gorbachev was routinely greeted warmly by the pontiff whenever the former arrived in Rome as a private citizen. Gorbachev went on record calling the pope the "world's number one humanist." And John Paul described the former Soviet premier as "a brave soldier who made hard choices for his people, his country, and his world." John Paul was known to pray for Gorbachev and entertained the former premier not only at the Vatican but also as Castel Gandolfo, the papal summer residence outside of Rome. As well, Gorbachev through the years, in his speeches and writings, increasingly cited and quoted from the works and sayings of John Paul, describing him as a "major influence on all thoughtful men and women of the late twentieth century." He said, "Whether or not one lays claim to the Catholic faith, one is hard put not to look upon the Holy Father as a great moral leader, a force of courage, and a man of profound historical and philosophical importance. Few in their time have left such a mark as he." It can be argued that, coming from as large a personage as Mikhail Gorbachev—himself with no small amount of historical significance—this represents high praise indeed.

Interestingly, in a Boston speech delivered to computer professionals just days after John Paul II's 2005 death, Gorbachev called upon America's information technology (IT) leaders to learn a lesson from the late pope and extend their tools and expertise to impoverished corners of the world. Advocating John Paul II's view that the rich have an obligation to help the poor, Gorbachev called on the IT industry and on U.S. leaders to develop partnerships with other nations, including Russia. "Let us think not only about maximizing profits; let us think about the benefits for the future; let us think about future generations," said Gorbachev, picking up a theme that John Paul himself came to emphasize once Communism was done for.

CHAPTER

6

Traveling Pope

IF JOHN PAUL II SAW COMMUNISM AS THE FIRST AND GREATEST THREAT to the salvation of the world and the redemption of mankind—which he did—then he saw the materialism and self-indulgence of the rich West as Communism's close second. After the fall of the Soviets, the materialistic and decadent West remained to be dealt with in the pope's view. John Paul criticized the West's selfishness and secularism, and suggested, during one of his several trips to the United States, that the country lower its standard of living and share the balance of its wealth with the third world. (In the final analysis he viewed pure capitalism and pure Communism as flip sides of the same coin. "This world," he once said, "is not capable of making man happy." Only God could do that.)

From 1991 through the remainder of his life, one of his key focuses would be to encourage the affluent "first world" to aid the impoverished developing countries in substantive ways that brought up their standard of living without increasing the decadence of their citizens, and to recognize, as he once put it, "the intrinsic life and work of every human being." Concurrently, he also worked to heal both present-day rifts and ancient breaches between various societies and cultures—most important, to his mind, the rift between Christianity and Judaism.

These concerns caused him to become the first truly digital pope of the modern age, leveraging twentieth-century (and later twenty-first-century) technologies for outreach via Vatican TV, radio, and other outlets. These concerns likewise inspired him to travel far more widely and energetically than any pope in history, beyond Rome and far beyond his native Poland.

In the 2,000-year history of the church, no other pope journeyed as many pilgrimage miles as did John Paul II. Fluent in eight languages, John Paul visited more than 100 countries and every continent but Antarctica. During each excursion, he made it a point to see not only world and church leaders, but also the residents of hospitals, madhouses, slums, and prisons. "Paul VI had made a number of trips to other countries [but] he just never had that charisma . . . and those number of people [who came to see him]," recalled ABC News Vatican correspondent Bill Blakemore, who covered Pope John Paul II during his entire 26-year papacy. "John Paul, when he traveled, pulled out these enormous crowds believed to be the largest crowds ever yet assembled on Earth."

Everywhere he went, he conducted enormous, open-air Masses. Always he brought a message of economic justice and conciliation, combined with ecumenical tolerance, but he also always brought a message of theological and sexual conservatism. In 1997, during a homily at a large open-air Mass in Brazil, John Paul entered into an ongoing Brazilian political debate when he announced that the institution of the family was threatened by abortion and marital infidelity. The Roman Catholic leader also made a veiled attack on gay and lesbian

Riding in the popemobile, Pope John Paul II blesses the people in the Nigerian capital of Abuja on March 23, 1998. More than any pope in history, John Paul II traveled all over the world to connect with Catholic worshippers of many nations.

marriages. "Marital fidelity and respect for life in all phases of its existence are subverted by a culture that doesn't admit the transcendent nature of man, created in the image and likeness of God," he told delegates to a conference on family issues. "Among the truths obscured in the hearts of men by growing secularism and rampant hedonism, those regarding the family have come under particular attack," he said. In his address, the pope also insisted that sexual "diversity" should not be recognized when it comes to marriage, an obvious reference to gay and lesbian marriages, which John Paul stridently opposed. At the time that John Paul spoke, Brazil, the world's largest Catholic country, was in the throes of a heated national discussion over whether abortion should be made more readily available. In response to John Paul's comments, Brazil's first lady, Ruth Cardoso, went on the record saying John Paul should not seek to influence the debate.

John Paul carried the same combined messages of economic justice and theological and sexual conservatism, as well
as messages against the death penalty and war, to such outposts
as Costa Rica, Nicaragua, Panama, El Salvador, Guatemala,
Belize, Honduras, and Haiti (1983); India (1986 and 1999);
Togo, the Ivory Coast, Cameroon, Central African Republic,
Zaire, Kenya, and Morocco (1985); Zimbabwe, Botswana,
Lesotho, Swaziland, Mozambique, and South Africa (1988);
and Madagascar, Réunion, Zambia, and Malawi (1989).

Pope John Paul II's trips usually involved his efforts to
reach out to people of other faiths. The most ecumenical and
tolerant man ever to sit upon the Throne of St. Peter, John
Paul made it his business to cultivate good relations with a
range of religions: not only Christian Protestant churches and
Eastern Orthodox sects, but also Muslims, Jews, Buddhists, and
other variants on the theological theme. John Paul's outreach
to these churches operated on two levels. On the one hand, he
indicated that he sought a measure of communion with all the
major established faiths in the world. On the other, he made it
clear that, in his view, only the one Holy Roman and Apostolic
Catholic Church constituted faith in its truest and purest form.
John Paul insisted that only the church he oversaw as pontiff
was blessed divinely and completely by God. As far as he was
concerned, other religions could only find their faith by honoring to the rule of the Vatican and absorbing the catechism of
the Catholic Church.

Given this, every overture John Paul made to religions
beyond the Vatican contained a subtext of missionary work,
of bringing errant believers into true communion with God.
Many recipients of John Paul's outreach found this attitude not
only confusing, but also insulting. And John Paul himself often
misstepped. For example, in 1994, after more than a decade of
earnestly courting friendship with the world's Buddhists, the
pope put himself on record as describing Buddhism as being
mostly an atheistic system. Thereafter, the Vatican was forced

to issue a series of press releases reiterating the pope's profound respect for his "friend" the Dali Lama and other Buddhist leaders. Likewise, John Paul's earnest and heartfelt outreach to Jews worldwide suffered when he insisted on cultivating former Nazi Kurt Waldheim, the onetime Secretary General of the United Nations and eventual president of Austria. That same outreach absorbed another blow when John Paul defied Jewish public opinion and canonized Edith Stein, a Jew who converted to Catholicism, became a Carmelite nun, and was murdered at Auschwitz in August 1942 on account of her Jewish blood. In the eyes of most Jews, Stein was a Jew and was killed because of that. They did not understand why John Paul would declare her a martyr of the church, and were offended by the claim. John Paul similarly offended many Jews when he beatified Pius XII, a pope whom virtually all historians faulted for his willingness to accept Hitler and his failure to raise objections in the face of the Holocaust.

One of John Paul's first great efforts in ecumenism was the World Day of Prayer for Peace, which took place at Assisi, Italy, in 1986. There, in the Basilica of St. Francis, Jews, Buddhists, Christian Protestants, Shintoists, Muslims, Zoroastrians, Hindus, and practitioners of traditional African and Native American religions gathered to join their voices in a theme all could agree on. Sixteen years later, several months following the September 11 terrorist attacks made in the name of Islam and the God of Islam, the pope convened yet another such gathering at Assisi, at which representatives from each of the world's major religions collaborated in composing an ecumenical document condemning all forms of violence transacted in the name of any religion of any kind.

By the time of the 1986 conference in Assisi, John Paul II already had a long history of outreach to the Islamic world. Like Christians and Jews, the world's Muslims cited Abraham as the rock upon which they built their faith. In August 1985, during a visit to Morocco as the guest of King Hassan II,

Religious leaders from around the world gather in Assisi, Italy, to join Pope John Paul II in prayer during the World Day of Prayer for Peace on October 27, 1986.

John Paul met with thousands of Muslim youths in a sports stadium at Casablanca. Speaking Spanish into a microphone, his low baritone voice echoing across the stands, he reminded them: "we believe in the same God, the one God, the living God." However, it would be another sixteen years before John Paul made another brave step in Muslim/Vatican relations, by becoming the first pontiff to enter a mosque—the Umayyad mosque in Damascus, Syria. Tellingly, in the midst of his tour of the house of worship, the John Paul paused to pray only once: at a memorial to St. John the Baptist. Throughout the rest of his visit, televised to much of the Muslim world, John Paul seemed to display all the reverence of a sightseer. The ornate building, his body language made clear, was not especially holy.

Very early in his papacy, the pope formally apologized to Muslims for the medieval church-authorized and Vatican-financed wars of plunder called the Crusades. At the same time, however, he insisted that Muslims should leave behind their similar medieval intolerance: an intolerance that still lingered in so many Muslim-dominated states. He bemoaned, for example, the fact that both Christianity and Judaism were banned outright among natives of Saudi Arabia, and that the mere possession of a Judeo-Christian Bible could land a Saudi citizen in prison. In the same vein, during a trip to the Sudan, John Paul severely criticized the recent murder of a bishop and several Catholic missionaries in nearby Algeria, angering his hosts but never refraining from speaking truth to power.

Traveling to Israel in 2000 as the guest of Prime Minister Ehud Barak, John Paul made significant inroads in his over-tures to the Jews of the world while also insisting on the rights of Palestinians in the Middle East. During a stop at Bethlehem, where he paused to pray at a church built above the traditional birthplace of Jesus, the pontiff urged understanding between Israelis and the Palestinians. In the midst of the same trip, he restated his longstanding belief in Israel's right to exist but also said Palestinians deserved autonomy and self-rule.

As previously noted, anti-Semitism had long been a fun-damental component of Catholicism up through the early twentieth century. Young Wojtyla noted and disdained the anti-Semitism that pervaded his Catholic boyhood in Poland. Nevertheless, Catholic anti-Semitism had been very real and very vibrant for centuries. Jews were condemned by the church as the killers of Christ, sentenced to roam the Earth stateless and homeless until they accepted Christ's divinity. In 1904, before John Paul II was born, Theodore Herzl, the founding father of the modern Zionist movement, visited Pope Pius X, whom he asked to endorse the idea of a Jewish state in Palestine. Instead of encouragement, Herzl received brutal confirmation of ancient church doctrine. Pius reiterated the church's belief that Jews must remain without a homeland. At the end of their conversation he told Herzl, "We can't prevent Jews from going to Jerusalem, but we can never sanction it. . . .The Jews have not recognized our Lord and we can not recognize the Jews."

While other modern popes had gradually stepped away from such dogmatic bigotry, it was left to John Paul II to make the ultimate leap. For example, in 1986 John Paul became the first pope in history to set foot inside Rome's Great Synagogue, an establishment located no more than two miles from Vatican Hill. He was also the first pope to visit the Western Wall of the old synagogue (the fabled "Wailing Wall") in Jerusalem. There, following Jewish custom, John Paul placed a written prayer between the stones: "God of our fathers, You chose Abraham and his descendants to bring Your name to the nations. We are deeply saddened by the behavior of those, who, in the course of history, have caused these children of Yours to suffer and, asking Your forgiveness, we wish to commit ourselves to genuine brotherhood with the people of the Covenant."

The people of the covenant. An important phrase, and a vitally important notion in John Paul's calculus of faith. The pope stated again and again in public remarks concerning the Jews and Judaism that, in his judgment, God never recanted his divine covenant with the Jewish people. Nothing in the New Testament, nothing in any of the Gospels, no utterance attributed to the historical Jesus Christ ever suggested that the Jewish people would ever be anything but blessed in the eyes of God. John Paul insisted that the Jews were "irrevocably the beloved of God." He cited the Jews as "elder brothers in faith"

Tibetan Buddhist spiritual leader the Dalai Lama meets with Pope John Paul II at the Vatican on October 28, 1999. Although the pope met with many leaders of Eastern religions, he denounced their religions as atheistic.

to Christians everywhere. In step with these sentiments, John Paul became the first pontiff to formally recognize the state of Israel, establishing full diplomatic relations between Israel and the Vatican in 1993.

John Paul's theological conservatism remained steadfast, however. Ecumenism and brotherhood of men under God was one thing. Abandonment or negotiation of dogma and the sacred mysteries of faith was quite another. Throughout all his outreach to Judaism and other churches worldwide, the pope remained insistent in his staunch belief that the one Holy Roman and Apostolic Church was just that: the only true church ordained by God through Jesus Christ. Thus he insisted that Catholics engaged in dialogue with other religions remain fundamentally true to their core beliefs and work to spread the Gospel. In 2000, he approved a controversial Vatican document specifically elucidating and emphasizing Jesus Christ's unique place as the one and only savior of humanity, restating the universal and absolute value of Christianity, and mourning the "gravely deficient situation" of all those—Jew, Hindu, Buddhist, Muslim, Eastern Orthodox, and Protestant alike—who choose to dwell, spiritually, outside the church of Rome.

In the final analysis, John Paul made it clear that—in his view—the one and only path to true reconciliation between Catholicism and "sister" faiths would lead to the sublimation and surrender of those faiths to the church of Rome. John Paul repeatedly pledged to continue to work with other church leaders for "full communion" between all peoples of God. However, he repeatedly also made it clear that it would be the other churches that would be required to conform to the strictures of Catholicism, rather than the other way around. So tolerant and wise in so many arenas, John Paul nevertheless never thought for a moment that the Roman Catholic Church and its "infallible" leader, the pope, might not have a monopoly on ultimate spiritual truth.

This dogmatism was to haunt and trouble the later years of John Paul's pontificate, causing fissures in the foundation of the church he held so dear and threatening its very structure. In the end, John Paul's unyielding, pious, conservative certainty about all matters of faith would prove his single greatest shortcoming as a leader of the faithful. More than a few of the shepherd's sheep would drift away, in search of a less theologically ferocious approach to God. In the end, not a few critics would wind up questioning John Paul's almost medieval certainty about the ultimate, absolute, and total righteousness of Roman Catholicism as compared to other faiths, and the need to maintain nearly medieval practices within the church.

7

Crisis in
the Church

AS WE HAVE SEEN, ALTHOUGH HE WAS LIBERAL WHEN IT CAME TO ISSUES OF
political freedom and economic justice, Pope John Paul II was
quite conservative and dogmatic when it came to matters of faith.
This led to what many consider to be a crisis in the church.

The church inherited by John Paul II in 1978 was an institution in flux. The church was in search of its modern identity.
John Paul II took it upon himself to define that identity by
looking backward into tradition. While he was "liberal" when it
came to such issues as the death penalty and economic justice,
John Paul defined himself as co-equally conservative on theological questions.

Early in his pontificate, John Paul II embarked upon the
restoration of core Church values. Within his first weeks, the
pope rejected all manner of modern innovations including
contraception and married priests. Concurrently, he silenced
Catholic scholars who sought to disagree with him.

"... THIS POPE BETRAYED THE [VATICAN II] COUNCIL NUMEROUS TIMES."

—Hans Küng,
writing in *Der Spiegel*

Hans Küng, the liberal Catholic philosopher, whom John Paul II sought to discipline on more than one occasion, summarized his impression of John Paul's legacy after the pope's death. Writing in *Der Spiegel*, Kung said: "... this Pope betrayed the [Vatican II] council numerous times. Instead of using the conciliatory program words 'Aggiornamento–Dialogue and Collegiality–ecumenical,' what's valid now in doctrine and practice is 'restoration, lectureship, obedience and re-Romanization.' The criteria for the appointment of a bishop is ... to be absolutely loyal to the party line in Rome. Before their appointment, their fundamental conformity is tested ... and they are sacrally sealed through a personal and unlimited pledge of obedience to the pope that is tantamount to an oath to the 'Fuhrer.'"

Other critics, like Margaret Steinfels, the editor of the Catholic magazine *Commonweal*, saw John Paul II as a polarizing figure, especially with regard to his accusing the United States and other industrialized nations of fostering a "culture of death." "I don't deny that there are many problems in the U.S. and the West," Steinfels commented a number of years ago, "but I don't think that calling it a 'culture of death' and the Church the 'Church of life' is a useful way of dealing with things. I disagree with his [John Paul II's] metaphors."

The pope also perplexed Steinfels and many others with his insistence that church doctrine continue to prohibit the ordination of women. In affirming his position in a letter to the bishops in 1994, John Paul wrote uncompromisingly, "This judgment is to be definitively held by all the Church's faithful."

Shortly after John Paul's death, Hugh Burns, a commentator and Dominican priest, expressed exasperation in trying to bring together the threads of this pope's legacy. "John Paul's pontificate, one of the longest in history, was one of great accomplishment as well as anomaly," Burns wrote. "The tireless champion of human rights who stood up to communist repression dealt harshly with independent voices in the Church. He apologized for more than a millennium of Catholic anti-Semitism, then canonized several individuals whose attitudes and actions toward Jews remain an embarrassment. . . . John Paul has left a more disciplined Catholic Church. It is a stronger player in the shaping of the 21st century. It is also more divided within, more wary of internal dialogue than a generation ago. [But] there is a crippling shortage of clergy, along with a growing call for married and women priests. The crisis of pedophilia has seriously compromised the Church's ability to address any sexual matters convincingly."

Many saw the problem of priestly abuse of children as emerging from John Paul's continued insistence on priestly celibacy, a long tradition within the church that John Paul saw as being targeted by a media conspiracy of "systematic propaganda which is hostile" to the church. "The vow of celibacy is a matter of keeping one's word to Christ and the Church," he wrote, "a duty and a proof of the priest's inner maturity; it is the expression of his personal dignity." In keeping with his conspiracy theory of a war on celibacy, John Paul urged priests to use "vigilance against the seductions of the world."

Speaking to a group of French bishops in 2004, John Paul said he considered priestly celibacy of "inestimable value" and appealed for the support that priests need to show that Christ gives full meaning to their lives. "In today's world, the question of ecclesiastical celibacy and chastity that derives from it continues to be, frequently, both for youth as for other faithful, a stumbling block, object of numerous misunderstandings in public opinion." During the audience, John Paul cited

Protesters in Boston speak out against the Catholic Church's sex abuse scandal and carry signs demanding the resignation of Cardinal Bernard Law. Pope John Paul II accepted Law's resignation in 2002.

the faithfulness of priests, "who in this way show the world that Christ and the mission can fulfill a life." Those lives, he said, were "a testimony of the absoluteness of God and a particularly fruitful participation in the building of the Church." In fact, John Paul said, "Chastity in celibacy has an inestimable value. It constitutes an important key for the spiritual life of priests, for their commitment in the mission, and for their appropriate pastoral relation with the faithful, which should not be based on emotional aspects, but on the responsibility of his ministry." For these reasons, the Holy Father invited priests "to be vigilant in the face of the seductions of the world and to make an examination of conscience regularly . . . Every attitude that goes against this teaching constitutes an anti-testimony for the Christian community and for all men." The Holy Father asked the bishops to support young priests especially who, like their contemporaries, "are characterized both by extraordinary enthusiasm as well as the frailties of their time. . . .Appropriate psychological and spiritual assistance can also be shown to be necessary so that situations will not last that, with the passing of time, could become dangerous."

Dangerous was right. The priest pedophilia scandals that emerged during the last decade of John Paul's reign rocked the Catholic Church and left many wondering if the very church itself, the leaders of which tried to lay the blame for the scandal not on celibacy but on homosexuality, did not have feet of clay. Many analysts and commentators also saw the celibacy rule as being the chief reason why the church's recruitment of new, young priests was so problematical during John Paul's papacy. Throughout the last two decades of the twentieth century, the world population of priests, and, for that matter, nuns, declined precipitously, forcing the closure of Catholic schools and the consolidation of Catholic churches worldwide.

In nearly all matters, the church seemed out of step with both the modern world and with its own parishioners. The majority of Catholics believed priests should be able to marry, that sensible family planning through contraception should be allowed, that the ordination of women made genuine sense, and that gays had a natural right to follow their own sexual instincts, just as heterosexuals did. John Paul, however, believed none of these things, just as he did not believe popular senti-ment among the faithful should be a factor in the Vatican's shaping and interpretation of doctrine.

Gays within the church, meanwhile, thought it ironic that the pope could reach out to practitioners of Islam but not to homosexuals struggling to find a place for themselves as Catholics. Marianne Duddy-Burke, of the Catholic gay rights group Dignity/Boston, commented after John Paul's death, "Obviously he had a very negative impact on [gay] Catholics, on our families, on social policy that's in real contrast with the many positive parts of his legacy that are obviously the focus of the remembrances this week. It was under this Pope that the language of 'objectively disordered' and 'intrinsically evil' as applied to gay and lesbian people emerged as sort of official Vatican policy. And the hatefulness of the rhetoric that came from Vatican officials, including the Pope himself, on issues of families headed by same-sex couples being violent to children, the scapegoating of gay priests for the sexual abuse scandals, and the attacks on countries that were working to find more justice under civil law for their [gay] citizens, all of this came under terrible attacks from the Vatican. I think the other sort of connected legacy is really the number of lives that were lost to the HIV/AIDS epidemic, not strictly among the gay community, but all across the world because of the Vatican's refusal and the Pope's refusal to even consider condom use as a lifesaving preventative measure. It just really diverges from his general concern for the poor. This was just a blind spot that was huge when you look at his overall impact on the world stage." (Visiting with Mother Teresa, whom he later beatified, in rampantly overcrowded India, the pope endorsed her advise to the young women who flocked to her clinic, that they be "open to life" and disdain family planning.)

On the issue of the ordination of female priests, John Paul also remained unyielding. In his arguments against, he cited Christ's recruitment of men only to form his group of apostles, the long tradition of male clerics throughout the history of the church, and the fact that even the Virgin Mary herself was not called to serve in a priestly manner. "Furthermore," he wrote in an encyclical, "the fact that the Blessed Virgin Mary, Mother of God and Mother of the Church, received neither the mission proper to the Apostles nor the ministerial priesthood clearly shows that the non-admission of women to priestly ordination cannot mean that women are of lesser dignity, nor can it be construed as discrimination against them. Rather, it is to be seen as the faithful observance of a plan to be ascribed to the wisdom of the Lord of the universe." (Nevertheless, he added, "The presence and the role of women in the life and mission of the Church, although not linked to the ministerial priesthood, remain absolutely necessary and irreplaceable.") Thus female Catholics who felt themselves called by God to serve in a priestly role, also soon found themselves called to Anglicanism or Methodism, or some other branch of Christianity willing to accept them as such. In the process, the Roman Catholic Church continued to lose significant numbers of parishioners (not to mention motivated talent) from its "faithful."

Meanwhile, of those who remained practicing Catholics, the vast majority tacitly denied the authority of the pope on at least some subjects. Most prominent among these was birth control. Of young practicing Catholic couples, more than 80 percent said in surveys that they practiced "unnatural" and therefore unauthorized family planning: condoms, birth-control pills, and other methods. Less than 20 percent relied upon the Vatican-authorized rhythm method of "natural" family planning. (At the same time, a joke began to circulate. *Question: What do you call people who practice the rhythm method of birth control? Answer: Parents.*) Concurrent with all this, many of the most thoughtful and serious young couples in the church, those most valuable to the institution in the long-term, chose to seek out other Christian denominations, where their sex lives and their religion would not need to collide, and where they would not have to feel like hypocrites.

Other liberal Catholics decided to try and remain in the church and work for change from within. During 1995 a group of lay and ordained Catholics in Innsbruck, Austria issued a church referendum to call for a more liberal, open, and inclusive Catholicism. Saying that they represented the "voices of the people in the pews," the members of We Are Church asked in their referendum that Rome "(1) equally respect all the people of God, whether lay or ordained, (2) grant full equal rights to

Gay activists stand in St. Peter's Square at the Vatican to protest Pope John Paul II's stance on homosexuality. Many people believe the Roman Catholic Church should be more progressive in its views on same-sex marriages, birth control, and marriage for priests.

women, (3) lift mandatory celibacy for priests, (4) encourage a positive understanding of sexuality, and (5) teach the gospel as a message of joy." This group soon spread throughout Europe and into North America. Today it has branches in no less than 20 countries. In the United States, the Association for the Rights of Catholics in the Church, Catholics for a Free Choice, and other such organizations rose up to protect and defend the spirit of the Second Vatican Council, and to lobby for modernization, liberality, and democracy within the ancient institution.

According to its charter, Catholics Speak Out "was born out of the belief that progressive Catholics, committed to the Gospel and the spirit of the Second Vatican Council, have been silent too long in the face of conservative trends. The organization says, "We rode the wave of euphoria which flowed from the Council, but we have been reluctant to speak out and struggle with those who would return the Church to its repressive past." Meanwhile, according to its Web site, the Association for the Rights of Catholics in the Church "was founded in 1980 by lay and clerical Catholics in the wake of Vatican condemnations of such theologians as Edward Schillebeeckx, Jacques Pohier, and Hans Küng." The ARCC seeks to "institutionalize a collegial and egalitarian understanding of the church in which decision making is shared and accountability is realized among Catholics of every kind." Other groups have similar charters. All question the traditional hierarchy of the church, the infallibility of the pope, and the autocratic nature of pronunciations from the Vatican. Each boasts a large membership of concerned Catholics committed to breathing new life into what they believe to be the musty, decaying body of Mother Church.

In his time, John Paul condemned each of these institutions as subversive to the word of Christ, and thus evil-inspired. He likewise threatened excommunication for those Catholics who participated in the organizations he found so troubling, organizations that grew apace Mother Church's diminishment. Critics referred to John Paul as a "reactionary in shepherd's clothing."

"The traditional religious orders, the Jesuits, Dominicans, and Franciscans, have been removed from the heart of the decision-making process," wrote Mexican journalist Alberto Aziz Nassif, "and their place has been taken by new orders and movements, with Opus Dei, the Legion of Christ, and other conservative religious organizations taking a leading role. With this there has been a shift toward conservative positions and a diminution of the role of progressive theologians. . . .We have a great contrast: a Pope who has used modern means to express himself, who has traveled the world over like no other Pope before him, who has placed the church in a new international position and transformed the religious landscape in a radical fashion, but one who, at the same time, has erected a wall of traditionalism against the challenges and problems of modernity, preached doctrines that urgently need revision, and governed the church by medieval means—a Pope who has surrounded himself with individuals, orders, and movements at the conservative end of the spectrum. This restoration is leaking on every front. Perhaps the pendulum of history will soon swing back to enable the church to find a way to deal with the problems of the 21st century—not from the prison of tradition but instead by interacting with the demands and necessities of a world that no longer fits the medieval mold in which the church has been kept these past 25 years."

8

Final Years

"IT IS WONDERFUL TO BE ABLE TO GIVE ONESELF TO THE VERY END FOR THE sake of the kingdom of God. At the same time, I find great peace in thinking of the time when the Lord will call me: from life to life," Pope John Paul II said in a 1999 letter addressed to the elderly. Describing the Pope in the fall of 1998, Cardinal Joseph Ratzinger stated: "The pain is written on his face. His figure is bent, and he needs to support himself on his pastoral staff. He leans on the cross, on the crucifix. . . ." In John Paul's final years, his step became unsure and the stoop of his back, bent years before when he was hit by a truck in Krakow, became more pronounced. Parkinson's Disease afflicted him severely. He endured colon surgery in 1992. One year later he dislocated a shoulder in a fall. The year 1994 brought another fall resulting in a broken femur. There was an appendectomy in 1996. The year 2003 brought an end to the pope's attempts to walk in public. Then, 2004 saw the last of his public liturgies. He

Cuban leader Fidel Castro hosts Pope John Paul II in Havana on January 25, 1998. The pope made a five-day pilgrimage to Communist Cuba and called for the creation of a new society offering "peace, justice, freedom."

always spoke bluntly, though, about his age, his failing health, and his oncoming death. John Paul said he was determined to stay in command of the church, but also said that he was ready for and happy to contemplate the new birth and life in heaven that awaited him.

The January 1998 papal trip to Cuba, where he was grandly and warmly welcomed by the atheist Fidel Castro, posed a sharp contrast to the robust, young John Paul's United States visit in 1979. Jack Wintz, a writer for *St. Anthony Messenger*, personally covered both John Paul's 1979 United States trip and the Cuba trip of 1998. Thus he had a firsthand experience of the enormous change in the pope's health. "In Cuba," wrote Wintz, "the Pope's athletic stamina was gone. His gait was slow and at times shuffling, his speech was often slurred and his hand sometimes trembled. But frankly, I felt there was something beautiful and noble in the Pope's witness. His courageous perseverance in carrying out his activities as Pope, despite his physical afflictions, was a heart-lifting example for all of us. This was, perhaps, doubly true for all those people around the globe who were themselves bearing some cross or affliction. Many of us, faced with the same tests, would be tempted to shrink from public view, as if infirmity were an embarrassment or personal disgrace. [But John Paul] bore his infirmities as if they were badges of honor and opportunities for imitating the courage of the suffering Christ. His humble, unpretentious and unembarrassed acceptance of suffering was a dramatic form of witness. The Pope offered the world a wonderful model for responding with grace to the test of suffering and illness. As Cardinal Ratzinger observed, John Paul II helps us realize that 'even age has a message . . .'"

Always, he philosophized about the suffering so often associated with old age. "Christ does not explain in the abstract the reasons for suffering," he pointed out in an essay, "but before all else he says: 'Follow me!' Come! Take part through your suffering in this work of saving the world. . . . Gradually, as the individual takes up his cross, spiritually uniting himself to the Cross of Christ, the salvific meaning of suffering is revealed before him." Elsewhere he wrote: "Your sufferings, accepted and borne with unshakeable faith, when joined to those of Christ take on extraordinary value for the life of the Church and the good of humanity." He also insisted that suffering could be transformed into something noble and good: "In the light of Christ's death and resurrection, illness no longer appears as an exclusively negative event . . . rather, it is seen as . . . an opportunity to release love . . . to transform the whole of human civilization into a civilization of love."

John Paul's decline did not slow his political activism. He disagreed with both presidents Bush on their wars against Iraq. "The Persian Gulf War in 1991, he opposed," remembers the

Rev. Richard McBrien, professor of theology at the University of Notre Dame. "And then the war in Iraq launched in 2003 . . . he also opposed that on moral grounds. He opposed the notion of pre-emptive war." During the months leading up to the U.S. attack on Iraq in 2003, John Paul repeatedly spoke out against the entire notion of a preemptive strike against Saddam Hussein. (At one point John Paul even sent his personal representative Cardinal Pio Laghi, an old friend of the Bush family, to make his case with the U.S. president, to no avail. In the same time frame, the pope sent a representative with a similar message to Saddam Hussein, and pointedly received Iraq's deputy prime minister, Tariq Aziz, at the Vatican. Once the war had been launched, John Paul's criticisms continued. Speaking to the audience of the Italian religious television channel, *Telespace*, the pontiff said: "When war, as in these days in Iraq, threatens the fate of humanity, it is ever more urgent to proclaim, with a strong and decisive voice, that only peace is the road to follow to construct a more just and united society. Violence and arms can never resolve the problems of man." Then, in January 2004, the pope made the following remarks to the diplomatic corps at the Vatican: "The many attempts made by the Holy See to avoid the grievous war in Iraq are already known. Today what matters is [to help the Iraqis regain] sovereignty and determine democratically a political and economic system that reflects their aspirations. . . ."

The elderly John Paul also continued to comment on topics related to economic justice, lecturing the Western "first world." In a speech delivered to diplomats at the Vatican on January 1, 2003, the pope criticized "all that impels man to protect himself inside the cocoon of a privileged social class or a cultural comfort which excludes others." He said, "The life-style of the prosperous, their patterns of consumption, must be reviewed in the light of their repercussions on other countries. Let us mention for example the problem of water resources, which the United Nations Organization has asked us all to consider during this year 2003. Selfishness is also the indifference of prosperous nations towards nations left out in the cold. All peoples are entitled to receive a fair share of the goods of this world and of the know-how of the more advanced countries. How can we fail to think here, for example, of the access of everyone to generic medicines, needed to continue the fight against current pandemics, an access—alas—often thwarted by short-term economic considerations?"

That same year, 2003, during an autumn visit to Slovakia, John Paul seemed to collapse from exhaustion before he was halfway through his prepared remarks. This episode led the pope's handlers to cut back his travel schedule greatly. The highlights of his travel for 2004 included brief excursions to sites convenient to the Vatican, such as Lourdes and Switzerland. February 2005 found the pontiff hospitalized with a severe respiratory ailment, one that eventually led to a tracheotomy procedure and the insertion of a breathing tube. At this time, John Paul authorized an aide to transact his weekly Angelus blessing, a signal that he was starting to let go of this world. On Easter Sunday (March 27) John Paul was rolled to his Vatican window. Below him, an eager crowd in St. Peter's Square awaited his blessing. With an assistant holding a microphone to his lips, the pope tried desperately to shape the words "in the name of the father," but in the end both he and the faithful had to settle for a silent blessing, the pope mustering every ounce of his waning energy to wave his hand weakly in the sign of the cross. His final public appearance in the same window three days later, the Wednesday before his death, produced an equally frustrating result.

Friday, April 1, saw John Paul II lapse into his final crisis. Sequestered in his Vatican apartment, he remained conscious and, according Vatican spokesman Joaquin Navarro-Valls, "extraordinarily serene." Slowly, through the day, the process of death overtook the pontiff's body. One by one, his organs began to shut down as his pulse faded and his breathing became

As is evident from this photo taken on October 17, 2004, Pope John Paul II suffered physically in his last years, requiring assistance to kneel, sit, and stand.

shallow. Doctors and nurses kept him comfortable, but exerted no extraordinary effort to keep him alive. While the medical professionals tinkered, a common priest accompanied by several Polish nuns prayed near the pope's bedside, the priest having earlier that day said Mass, in which the pope participated. Speaking via the press that afternoon, Cardinal Camillo Ruini, vicar of Rome, asked that all the faithful intensify their prayers. "The pope," he announced, "is completely abandoned to the will of God."

Saturday morning found the pontiff lapsing in and out of consciousness. During an intermittent moment of clarity, he dictated a message for the prayerful crowd of 70,000 gathered outside: "I have looked for you. Now you have come to me. And I thank you." A few hours later, as evening settled, word came that John Paul had passed away. Without prompting, the faithful in St. Peter's Square began a round of applause that seemed might never stop. Only a request that echoed out over loudspeakers—the same loudspeakers that had so often carried the blessings of John Paul—settled them down. Church officials asked for silence, so that all assembled might "accompany the pope in his first steps to heaven."

In the final analysis, there has never been a pope who has so successfully translated his personal strength, determination, and faith into such widespread respect and goodwill. In a world of shifting trends and leaders of questionable virtue, John Paul II proved, even to those who did not agree with him in all things, to be a towering figure at the moral center of modern-day life. His moral compass, whether one agreed with it or not, was unwavering and did not shift with the winds of popular opinion. This was not a pope who looked at opinion polls. This was a pope who acted from deep conviction derived from a devout life of contemplation and prayer. Right or not, he was always, in the most elemental sense, well-meaning and true.

It was that good and true spirit whom church activists, even before John Paul II's body was placed in the ground below St.

Peter's, began to speak of as a potential saint. Indeed, the first steps toward sainthood began within days of John Paul II's last breath. Within months, John Paul II's successor, Pope Benedict XVI—the former Cardinal Ratzinger of Germany—announced that, with regard to John Paul, he would dispense with rules that normally impose a five-year waiting period before beatification. (John Paul himself set the precedent in 1999 when he granted a dispensation and let Mother Teresa's sainthood cause start just two years after her death.) Now the faithful await miracles. Vatican procedures in place for some 500 years require one miracle for someone to be beatified and a second to be canonized. But as Cardinal Darío Castrillón Hoyos observed recently, "There's no lack of miracles, he performed many while he was still alive."

Saint or not, John Paul II left an indelible mark on history, on contemporary society, and on his church. As *Newsday's* Bob Keeler wrote: "Like few other leaders, religious or secular, Pope John Paul II took the last quarter of the century in his strong Polish hands and shook it, laboring to retain doctrinal discipline in his church and helping to plant the seeds of the movement that liberated his native land from Communism. . . . Admirers and critics alike agreed that he made a powerful impact. 'I think he embodies this century more than any other man' the late Jonathan Kwitny said in a *Newsday* interview in 1996. . . . 'He lived through the most momentous events of the century—at the beginning involuntarily, later on quite voluntarily—and he has confronted all of the issues of the century.'"

For the immediate future, John Paul's church seems destined to remain stuck in a deep quagmire of ancient theological orthodoxy. The bishops and cardinals he so carefully selected through his decades in power are all of his same conservative stripe when it comes to matters of faith. In turn, they will themselves promote like-minded younger men. Thus the strenuous work of John Paul II will be felt at the Vatican, and in every Catholic church, for generations to come. Whether this is a good thing,

Pope John Paul II is photographed on his papal throne on May 16, 1990, during his weekly general audience. Because of the pope's remarkable reign, his successor, Benedict XVI, has called for an early beatification.

and whether this will accrue to the benefit of Catholicism and mankind, remains to be seen. But the fact of John Paul's ongoing and robust presence in the affairs of this world and the affairs of the church cannot be denied.

But when asked about the old comrade he still sometimes calls Lolek, Jerzy Kluger speaks not of a world leader, nor of a pope, nor of a saint in the making. "I just miss my friend," he said. "I just miss the good boy who grew up to be a good man— the boy who always loved me, and I him. It is that simple. I miss Karol who kicked the soccer ball so well, who climbed the mountains so high, who wrote the beautiful poetry, and who welcomed me always to his home, whether it was a tiny apartment in Poland or a giant palace atop Vatican Hill. He often—so often—spoke about the Jews being brothers in faith to the Christians. Well, he was my brother. That I know. He was my brother always, and I his. Now I miss him, but I am glad his sufferings are over, and that he has laid down his cross. I think I will see him again, healthy, smiling, in God."

CHRONOLOGY

1920	Born Karol Wojtyla on May 18 in Wadowice, Poland.
1929	Mother dies.
1932	Older brother Edmund dies.
1938	Karol and his father move to Krakow; Karol enters Jagellonian University, and joins theater group.
1940	Karol interrupts studies to work as a laborer after Nazi invasion of Poland in 1939.
1941	Karol's father dies.
1942	Karol enters secret seminary in Krakow; two years later he goes into hiding to avoid arrest by the Nazis.
1945	Karol resumes his studies at Jagellonian University.
1946	After being ordained as a priest, Karol takes up graduate studies in Rome.
1948	Completes doctorate in theology.
1949	Named assistant pastor of a parish in Poland.
1953	Teaches ethics at Jagellonian University.
1954	Starts teaching philosophy at the Catholic University of Lublin; earns his second doctorate, this time in philosophy.
1958	Appointed auxiliary bishop of Krakow.
1960	*Love and Responsibility* hits bookstores and becomes an influential best seller.
1962	Attends first session of the Second Vatican Council in Rome.
1963	Attends second session of the Second Vatican Council, and is appointed archbishop of Krakow (installed 1964).
1964	Attends third session of the Second Vatican Council.
1965	Attends final session of the Second Vatican Council, and helps draft a key Vatican II document on the church and the modern world.
1967	Appointed cardinal.

1978	Elected 264th pope and bishop of Rome.
1979	Visits numerous countries including the Dominican Republic, Mexico, Poland, Ireland, the United States, and Turkey; ratifies a Vatican declaration rebuking Swiss-born Catholic theologian Father Hans Küng.
1980	Convenes special synod to address problems in Dutch church, largely in response to liberal influences of which he does not approve.
1981	Receives nearly fatal gunshot wounds during an assassination attempt in St. Peter's Square; names Cardinal Joseph Ratzinger, who would one day succeed him as pope, head of Vatican doctrinal congregation.
1982	Marks anniversary of assassination attempt by visiting the holy sites at Fatima, Portugal; meets with Palestinian leader Yasser Arafat.
1983	Visits his would-be assassin, Mehmet Ali Agca, in prison, and issues forgiveness.
1984	Visits World Council of Churches headquarters in Geneva.
1985	Calls for a special bishops' synod to review the two decades since Vatican II.
1986	Visits Rome's main synagogue; calls leaders of the world's diverse religions to Assisi to pray for peace; continues to repress dissent among Catholic theologians.
1987	Calls major Vatican meeting to resolve Catholic-Jewish controversies; makes second visit to United States.
1988	Issues a major and controversial encyclical, "On Social Concerns," chastising the "First World" for ignoring the "Third World"; drafts papal letter defending women's

equality and key role in Catholicism, but insists at the same time they can never be ordained priests.

1989 Hailed as a major hero in the collapse of Soviet communism.

1990 Promulgates strict global norms for Catholic higher education; approves Vatican instruction further tightening the range on theological dissent within the ranks of the church.

1991 Orchestrates a special European synod to discuss the rapid changes taking place on that continent after communism's collapse.

1992 Undergoes surgery for removal of non-cancerous colon tumor; issues revised official "Catechism of the Catholic Church"; receives and approves a Vatican report stating that the church was wrong in condemning Galileo.

1993 Makes third U.S. visit for World Youth Day; writes seminal papal encyclical on the nature of moral theology.

1994 Reiterates that the church decision against priesthood for women will never change; arranges for the Vatican to exchange ambassadors with Israel; publishes the best seller *Crossing the Threshold of Hope*.

1995 Issues major encyclicals on reverence for human life and the nature of ecumenism.

1996 Urges total, worldwide ban on both nuclear testing and land mines.

1997 Presides at *Synod for America*.

1998 Visits Cuba and is personally hosted by Fidel Castro; begins important, ongoing Catholic-Muslim dialogue.

1999	Unseals the "Holy Door" in St. Peter's Basilica to start jubilee year 2000.
2000	Visits Holy Land.
2001	Becomes first pope to enter a mosque.
2002	Convenes yet another ecumenical day of prayer for peace in Assisi; visits Toronto for World Youth Day.
2003	Beatifies Mother Teresa of Calcutta after expediting her path to sainthood.
2004	Publishes *Rise, Let Us Be on Our Way*.
2005	Publishes *Memory and Identity: Conversations Between Millenniums*; dies April 2.

BIBLIOGRAPHY

Bernstein, Carl, and Marco Politi. *His Holiness: John Paul II and the Hidden History of Our Time.* New York: Doubleday, 1996.

Craig, Mary. *Man from a Far Country: An Informal Portrait of Pope John Paul II.* New York: William Morrow & Co., 1979.

Hogan, Richard, and John Levoir. *Covenant of Love: Pope John Paul II on Sexuality, Marriage, and Family in the Modern World.* New York: Doubleday, 1985.

Kwitny, Jonathan. *Man of the Century: The Life and Times of John Paul II.* New York: Henry Holt, 1997.

O'Connor, Gary. *Universal Father: A Life of John Paul II.* New York: Bloomsbury, 2005.

Szulc, Tad. *Pope John Paul II: The Biography.* New York: Scribner, 1995.

Weigel, George. *Witness to Hope: The Biography of Pope John Paul II.* New York: HarperCollins, 1999.

FURTHER READING

Baumgartner, Frederic J. *Behind Locked Doors: A History of the Papal Elections.* New York: Palgrave Macmillan, 2003.

John Paul II, Pope. *Letter of the Pope to Children in the Year of the Family.* Boston: St. Paul Editions, 1994.

——. *Love and Responsibility.* Trans. H.T. Willetts. New York: Farrar, Straus, Giroux, 1981.

——. *To the Youth of the World.* Boston: St. Paul Editions, 1985.

——. *The Word Made Flesh: The Meaning of the Christmas Season.* Trans. Leslie Wearne. New York: Harper & Row, 1985.

Keating, Karl. *What Catholics Really Believe.* Ft. Collins, Colo.: Ignatius Press, 1995.

Kreeft, Peter. *Catholic Christianity: A Complete Catechism of Catholic Beliefs Based on the Catechism of the Catholic Church.* Ft. Collins, Colo.: Ignatius Press, 2001.

LoBello, Nino. *The Incredible Book of Vatican Facts and Papal Curiosities: A Treasury of Trivia.* Liguori, Mo.: Liguori Publications, 1998.

Schreck, Alan. *Catholic and Christian: An Explanation of Commonly Misunderstood Catholic Beliefs.* Cincinnati: Servant Publications, 1984.

Williams, George Huntston. *The Mind of Pope John Paul II.* New York: The Seabury Press, 1981.

PHOTO CREDITS

INDEX

ordination of women, 78, 81, 82–83

papal elections, 46–50
Paul VI (pope), 40, 42, 45, 46
pedophilia scandals, 13, 79, 81
Persian Gulf War, 89
Pio, Father Fancesco Forgione, 35
Pius XII (pope), 35, 38, 70
Pius X (pope), 73
plays written by Wojtyla, 28, 42
Poland
   anti-Nazi resistance in, 29, 36
   German occupation of, 28–32, 36
   John Paul II visits, 56–59
   Russian "liberation" of, 32
   struggle for democracy in, 59–63
Polish Catholic Church
   government persecution of, 37–38
   opposition of Polish Communism by, 40–42
   people's devotion to, 41
   Wyszynski appointed archbishop, 35–36
Polish government
   oppression of Catholic Church by, 37–38, 40–42
   Solidarity banned by, 62
   telegram to Pope upon election, 55
   Wojtyla's dealings with as archbishop, 40–42
Polish Independent Syndicate Solidarnosc (Solidarity Union), 59–63
Politi, Marco, 30
popes, election of, 46–50. *See also names of specific popes, e.g.,* Paul VI

priests
   celibacy of, 79–81
   child sexual abuse scandals, 13, 79, 81
   decline in numbers of, 81
   women as, 78, 81, 82–83
professorship at Catholic University of Lublin, 38

Ratzinger, Cardinal Joseph, 19–20, 87, 94
Reagan, Ronald, 63
Reese, Thomas J., 46
religions, non-Catholic, 69–75
religious education. *See* theological education
Rigali, Cardinal Justin, 18
Roman Catholic Church. *See* Catholic Church
Romania, 63
Romano Pontifici Eligendo, 46
Rome, postgraduate studies at, 33–35
Ruini, Cardinal Camillo, 93
Russia. *See also* Soviet Union
   Gorbachev reforms in, 62
   liberation of Poland by, 32

sainthood, 94
saints. *See names of specific saints, e.g.,* Stanislaw, Saint
Sandri, Archbishop Leonardo, 14–15
Sapieha, Archbishop Adam Stefan, 30, 31, 32, 37
Second Vatican Council, 38–40, 53, 84
seminary education, 30, 32, 38
Seminary of Krakow, 38
sexual abuse of children by priests, 13, 79, 81

sexuality, Church policies on, 68,
81–82
Silvestrini, Cardinal Achille, 14
smoke signal in election of pope,
48
Solidarity Union, 59–63
Somalo, Cardinal Eduardo Marti-
nez, 14
Soviet Communist Party, 59
Soviet Union. *See also* Russia
dissolution of, 63
Gorbachev reforms in, 62
rebellions in bloc nations, 62–63
St. Florian's Church, 36
St. Peter's Square funeral proces-
sion, 16
Stanislaw, Saint, 58
Stein, Edith, 70
Steinfels, Margaret, 78
Styczen, Father Tadeusz, 52
suffering, meaning of, 89
Szulc, Tad, 33, 37, 53, 59

Teresa, Mother, 82
theater, Wojtyla's interest in, 28
theological conservatism of John
Paul II, 13–14, 53–54, 75–79,
85–86
theological education, 30, 32,
33–35, 36, 37
travels, 67–69, 72, 88–89, 91
Tyranowski, Jan, 30

UNIA, 29

Vatican II. *See* Second Vatican
Council
Vatican policies. *See* Catholic

Church doctrines
via negative, 30
viewing of body, 16–17
voting, in papal election, 46–47,
48–49

Wadowice, Poland, 23, 32
Waldheim, Kurt, 70
Walesa, Lech, 59–60, 62
We Are Church, 83–84
Western materialism, 66, 90–91
Wiesel, Elie, 13
Wintz, Jack, 88
Wojtyla, Edmund (brother), 23, 26
Wojtyla, Emilia Kaczorowska
(mother), 23, 26
Wojtyla, Karol (father), 23, 26–28,
29
women, ordination of, 78, 81,
82–83
World Day of Prayer for Peace, 70
world leaders at funeral, 17–18, 20
world opinion at death, 12–13
writings
The Acting Person, 42
Crossing the Threshold of Hope,
63
dissertations, 35, 36, 42
*Evaluation of the Possibility of
Constructing a Christian Ethic
Based on the System of Max Sche-
ler*, 42
In Front of the Jeweler's Shop, 42
Love and Responsibility, 38, 42
Wyszynski, Bishop Stefan, 35–36

Yeltsin, Boris, 63
youth, 28–32

ABOUT THE AUTHORS

EDWARD J. RENEHAN, JR., is the author of books that include *Dark Genius of Wall Street: The Misunderstood Life of Jay Gould, King of the Robber Barons* (2005), *The Kennedys at War* (2002), *The Lion's Pride* (1998), *The Secret Six* (1995), and *John Burroughs: An American Naturalist* (1992). He lives in Rhode Island with his wife and two children.

ARTHUR M. SCHLESINGER, JR. is the leading American historian of our time. He won the Pulitzer Prize for his books *The Age of Jackson* (1945) and *A Thousand Days* (1965), which also won the National Book Award. Professor Schlesinger is the Albert Schweitzer Professor of the Humanities at the City University of New York and has been involved in several other Chelsea House projects, including the series *Revolutionary War Leaders, Colonial Leaders*, and *Your Government*.